CHOSEN VESSELS

Chosen Vessels

*Portraits of Ten Outstanding
Christian Men*

Edited by Charles Turner

VINE
BOOKS

Servant Publications
Ann Arbor, Michigan

Copyright © 1985 by Servant Publications

Cover illustration © 1985 by Jim Lamb
Book design by John B. Leidy

Published by Vine Books
P.O. Box 8617
Ann Arbor, Michigan 48107

Vine Books is an imprint of Servant Publications
designed to serve Evangelical Christians.

Printed in the United States of America
ISBN 0-89283-226-6

85 86 87 88 89 90   10 9 8 7 6 5 4 3 2 1

Library of Congress Cataloging in Publication Data

Chosen Vessels.

Contents: C.S. Lewis / by Harry Blamires—Paul
Brand / by Philip Yancey—William Wilberforce / by
Charles Colson—[etc.]
   1. Christian biography—Addresses, essays,
lectures. I. Turner, Charles, 1930—
BR1700.2.C48 1985   209'.2'.   85-14568
ISBN 0-89283-226-6

CONTENTS

Contributors

∽ **Harry Blamires** started writing in the late 1940s at the encouragement of his friend C.S. Lewis, his tutor at Oxford. His best-known books include *The Christian Mind* and *On Christian Truth*. He is also the author of three novels, *The Devil's Hunting-Grounds*, *Cold War in Hell*, and *Highway to Heaven*.

∽ **Robert E. Coleman** is Director of the School of World Evangelism at Trinity Evangelical Divinity School. His books include *The Master Plan of Evangelism*, *The Mind of the Master*, *Songs of Heaven*, and *The New Covenant*.

∽ **Charles Colson** holds degrees from Brown University and George Washington University. From 1969 to 1973 he served as Special Counsel to President Richard M. Nixon. Colson is president and founder of Prison Fellowship. His books include *Loving God*, *Born Again*, and *Life Sentence*. Mr. Colson's associate Ellen Santilli Vaughn collaborated on his chapter in *Chosen Vessels*.

∽ **Thomas Howard** is author of several books, including *Evangelical is Not Enough*, *The Novels of Charles Williams*, and *The Achievement of C.S. Lewis*.

∽ **W. Phillip Keller** is best known for his devotional commentaries. In addition to *A Shepherd Looks at Psalm 23*, he has written *A Layman Looks at the Lord's Prayer*, *A Shepherd Looks at the Good Shepherd*, and *As a Tree Grows*.

∽ **Malcolm Muggeridge** is the former editor of *Punch* and the author of several books, including *Something Beautiful for God, Christ and the Media, Jesus Rediscovered,* and *Chronicles of Wasted Time.*

∽ **J.I. Packer** is the author of *Knowing God, Evangelism and the Sovereignty of God, Knowing Man,* and *Keep in Step with the Spirit,* as well as several other books. He was an editor of the *New Bible Dictionary* and *The Bible Almanac.* He is currently Professor of Systematic and Historic Theology at Regent College, in Vancouver, British Columbia.

∽ **R.C. Sproul** is president of Ligonier Valley Study Center and Professor of Systematic Theology and Apologetics at Reformed Theological Seminary. His books include *Reason to Believe, In Search of Dignity, Who Is Jesus?,* and a novel, *Johnny Come Home.*

∽ **Charles Turner** has published short stories in a number of magazines in the United States and Europe. He is the author of *The Celebrant,* a historical novel.

∽ **Philip Yancey** is editor-at-large for *Christianity Today.* His books include *Where Is God When It Hurts* and *Insight.* He is co-author, with Paul Brand, of *Fearfully and Wonderfully Made* and *In His Image.*

Preface

SAINT PAUL WAS GOD'S "chosen vessel" to bear the name of Christ to the world. He was a container, an instrument, a conduit. He was a filled man, a missionary, a means of grace. He was an example of what every Christian ought to be. Having been knocked from his arrogance by the glory of the Risen Christ, he was a changed man who was fit for the Sovereign's use. Today we are still instructed through his ministry.

All of us who believe can call to mind other "chosen vessels" who have been agents of God in our lives. I don't restrict the term to those used by his Spirit in the conversion of an individual. The calling—for them, for all of us—is not to a cut-and-dried function that can be pinpointed that easily. We are to bear the name of Christ to the world and to each other in a continuing and integral action. We are to do it not only by speaking the word but by living it, not only by honoring the gospel in our writings but by adorning it in all kinds of practical ways. I suspect that Saint Paul made stronger, more attractive tents after his conversion than before, and that the workmanship of his seams bore the name of Christ as eloquently as did his tongue and reed.

This book is a celebration of the fact that God does choose human beings to channel his truth into the lives of other human beings. Ten examples are included, and they represent the diversity within the oneness of the Body of Christ. I am grateful to the authors who joined me in this project. Each of us has written about a man he highly esteems, a person from whom he has gained insights into the eternal.

Implicit in a grouping of Christian portraits like this is the Communion of the Saints. The Christian reader's identification with the subjects is not merely empathic. Between them is a kinship even deeper than that arising from common experience. They draw their true existence from the same source, from the one life that was sacrificed for the sins of many. If you and I are spiritually alive today, it is because we are recipients of a life that came out of the grave two thousand years ago. This is basic Christian belief. This indeed is what Christian life is, and it's well to remember that Christian life can never be isolated. It is united with its source by continuous flow and is necessarily lived in participation with all who have received this mystery.

So it is fitting that the portraits in this volume include the dead and the living. The Communion of the Saints, like the cross which validates it, stretches upward and outward. It embraces the redeemed of every age, the "cloud of witnesses" and the runners still on the track. I think we can be enriched by cultivating our relationships in the full Christian heritage, with those who now see him as he is and with those who still see through a glass darkly. I hope the readers of this book will get to know some outstanding "chosen vessels" who otherwise might have remained strangers. I hope all of us are reminded that we too are to be what Saint Augustine called "vehicles of Eternal Charity" in the lives of those around us and those who will follow.

The absence of women subjects herein is neither by slight nor oversight. *Bright Legacy* (Servant Publications, 1983) featured portraits of ten Christian women by ten Christian women. That book led the way for this one. We might say it was a matter of ladies first.

CHARLES TURNER

C.S. Lewis

by Harry Blamires

I RECALL CLEARLY C.S. Lewis' first words to me when I knocked on his door at Magdalen College and entered his room some time early in 1936. He looked me up and down and said, "Ah, good; an Anglo-Saxon. I've had nothing but Celts lately." Presumably he was referring to the succession of new pupils he was introducing himself to. Looking back now, and trying to recall what they looked like, I can see that my fair hair and pale complexion perhaps distinguished me. Certainly one of my year, Gerald Brodribb, who was later to become known as a writer on cricket, had a shock of red hair that flamed like a sunset. Lewis of course was just trying to make me feel comfortable by a personal remark that put the relationship on a companionable footing and was calculated to ease the natural awe of student for tutor. In my case he was never one hundred percent successful in this respect. Though years later I got on terms of real friendship with him, I never overcame the reluctance to be too familiar with one so distinguished. "My friends all call me Jack," he said, but if it was meant to be a hint or an invitation I didn't take it up. And Lewis' delicacy was such that he wouldn't force a change like that. In tune with the habits of the time he remained "Lewis" to me and I was "Blamires" to him.

Lots of people have described what it was like to be Lewis' pupil. One point ought to be mentioned—his meticulous conscientiousness. Illness apart, he was always there precisely on the tutorial hour and as ready to keep you till the time was up, sometimes till the next student knocked on the door. At a time when many tutors were notoriously lax and one heard stories of dons who practiced golf strokes on the carpet throughout tutorials or caught up with their correspondence while students read aloud their essays to the unresponsive furniture, this was a great boon to a student. It is especially worth mentioning because Lewis' own view of a university such as Oxford was that its fellows were meant to live the "clerkly life." They were there to study. This was their vocation, and it had once been a celibate vocation. Dons were not there primarily to teach. They were not "educators," for education by teaching was something that happened to you at school. Dons were primarily men and women at work on their own studies. Students were there to pick up whatever crumbs of enlightenment might be found by tagging on behind them. It is characteristic of Lewis that he held this ideal notion of a university don's function, yet in practice discharged his teaching obligations with punctilious care and thoroughness.

For he must often have been bored by the tedium of listening to third-rate essays read to him by uninspired students who wrote their weekly assignments by adapting chapters from *The Cambridge History of English Literature*. I myself was a fairly late developer. My earliest essays must have been drearily obvious to listen to. But I have no recollection at all of a bored-looking auditor, let alone of anything like a snub, a rebuke, or any remark that ever made me feel small. I remember only the occasional compliment, the word of praise that stimulated me enormously. I had been having tutorials with him for a couple of terms when he said, "You're beginning to ply a very pretty pen," and the remark has stayed in my mind ever since. I found throughout all my dealings with Lewis that if he wanted to draw attention to a fault, he would combine his criticism with praise for some quality or virtue. Once, when I had expressed myself very badly in a tutorial, replying very lamely and haltingly to his attempts to make me argue, he said: "You're like Oliver Goldsmith, as Dr. Johnson described him—

Here lies Nolly Goldsmith
For shortness called "Noll"
Who wrote like an angel
And talked like poor Poll.

Years later, when he took to pieces my first attempt to write a book in the field of literary criticism, his letter of analysis began: "You have struck gold and made a real critical advance." Then, after a paragraph in praise of what there was to praise, he settled down to a severe dissection of the book's faults. Lewis' careful consideration of the effect of his words on the person he was dealing with was a model of charity and sympathy in action. No man I have ever met was more anxious not to hurt others. When people talk about an overbearing Lewis or a bullying Lewis, they describe a man I never met.

Lewis was acutely conscious of the power of Christian personal influence in this respect—the use of words. (He was fond of saying, "The tongue is man's most unruly member, except one.") He once remarked to me, "Have you ever noticed how, when we angrily try to hurt people directly, especially when we want to make them feel small, our rebuke generally misfires; but when we are speaking quite innocently and charitably we may unintentionally touch their consciences and sting them? It's the unintended rebuke that stings. It's the same with praise," he added. His implication was that a watchful Providence restricts our capacity to do damage out of ill-will, for the very good reason that a rebuke bred of anger or envy is a tainted rebuke even if it happens in substance to represent a justifiable correction. But the same Providence may use our innocent, malice-free remarks to prick someone's conscience whom we are not trying to hurt.

I often reflected on these words. I found them especially apt because one of Lewis' most crucial practical influences on me was exercised in exactly this oblique way. Sometime in 1946 I completed a study of the English novel from its earliest beginnings up to the death of Sir Walter Scott in 1832, and I wrote to Lewis to ask if he would look through it. Overwhelmed though he must have been by demands at this time, he at once agreed. I had of course approached him apologetically. It was characteristic of Lewis that he did not make me feel that I was imposing a burden. "Most people just send their manuscripts without asking first," he wrote, "and I don't even know them." I was made to feel considerate for having been gracious enough to ask something with a polite preliminary letter! In my study I had tried to show how novelists, by their implicit moral attitudes, reflected changing emphases and in particular how a current of what Lewis himself called "the old Christian thought" surfaced in Scott's *Waverley Novels*. Lewis treated this manuscript with great thoroughness as he would have dealt with a doctoral thesis. He pencilled in marginalia. He put crosses where he thought a matter of fact or style was faulty. He put ticks where he thought a point merited approval. Two ticks and even three ticks marked a point that especially excited his approval.

I was studying this typescript one day when it suddenly struck me that the ticks tended to occur at places where I had been making judgments of a moral, theological, or philosophical character rather than sticking to my role as a literary critic. Noting this, I said to myself, "So perhaps that's the kind of writer I am really!" And so it was the influence of those ticks that gave me confidence to start writing as a lay theologian. What an apt illustration of Lewis' own theory that you may exercise the most compelling influence as a by-product of what you are consciously about.

To go back to Lewis as a tutor, I have no memories of anything but the maximum kindness and good-humor. Good-humor especially. There was a lot of laughing in Lewis' company. At that date he was a very cheerful man indeed. His tutorial method was to give you a reading assignment for a week. You had to produce an essay on it the next week to be read aloud to him and then dissected. He didn't give you a title for your essay. You must choose your own line. One of my most amusing tutorial experiences occurred after Lewis had told me to spend the week on the seventeenth-century poet and essayist, Abraham Cowley. Among Cowley's works was a massive neoclassical biblical epic, *The Davideis*, which is generally agreed to be a heavily uninspired effort in the genre of Milton's *Paradise Lost*. The time came for me to read my essay on Cowley to Lewis. There I sat in an armchair, my book on my knees, while Lewis faced me, sitting in the middle of his immense settee, pipe and tobacco on one side, a packet of Wills Goldflake cigarettes on the other side, and the two served his purposes alternately. As usual he held a paper and pencil in hand, the paper resting on the back of a book, so that he could jot down notes in preparation for dissecting my work afterwards. Halfway through my essay I launched on a thorough analysis of Cowley's epic, *The Davideis*. As I pursued my eloquent way through section after section of this vast work I gradually became conscious of a faint restlessness on Lewis' part. Soon he began to shake a little and then to rock from side to side. I had to look up and I found his face suffused with the largest and most uncontrollable grin I had seen there. I stopped reading. Vainly trying to smother his laughter, Lewis said, "You don't mean to say that you've actually *read* the thing!" "Every word," I said. His smile disappeared. The large face assumed a look of great solemnity and a note of deep compassion sounded in his voice. "I'm sorry," he said. "I'm terribly sorry," as if nothing could recompense me for his failure to warn me in advance against so outrageous a waste of my time. Then he visibly brightened. He had found a crumb of consolation. "But think," he said, pointing his finger at me, "you must be the only man in England, perhaps the only man alive, to have read every word of Cowley's *Davideis*."

Plainly Lewis did not believe in indiscriminate reading. On the other hand he did believe in repeated rereadings of what he most admired. As a student I once distinguished myself with an essay on

Malory's *Le Morte D'Arthur* which caused him to slap his knee as I finished reading and declare, "That's an alpha!" Some twelve years later when I came into his orbit as a young writer and we were talking about books, he said, "I remember a very good essay you wrote on Malory." I don't know now what I said in reply, but it must have conveyed to Lewis that Malory was not much in my thoughts at present, for he stiffened, stared me in the face, and assumed an expression of utter astonishment. "You don't mean to say you've *stopped* reading Malory!" Ruefully I had to confess that I was one of those philistines who, in spite of his patient tutelage, could allow a year to begin and end without opening *Le Morte D'Arthur*.

Was Lewis especially sympathetic to students who were evidently Christians? Not unfairly so in my experience. It is true that by a fluke I had read Lewis' *The Pilgrim's Regress* before I went up to Oxford in 1935. *The Pilgrim's Regress*, his first prose book, published by Dent in 1933, sold very badly. It was little known, even in Oxford. I could not at first find a fellow-student who had read it, or heard of it until I mentioned it. (After Sheed and Ward took it over from Dent I heard Lewis say that he had never received a penny for it—and this cannot have been said earlier than 1936.) But naturally, learning that Lewis was to be my tutor, I reread the book carefully, pencil in hand. I cannot now recall how or when I made clear to Lewis that I had read and enjoyed the book; but obviously a student does not conceal so useful a fact from his tutor for long. I mention this because it has occurred to me since that I may have been marked as the student who had read *The Pilgrim's Regress* long before I became the student who had read *The Davideis*. However that may be, there were occasions when, after the tutorial was over, I engaged Lewis in conversation on other matters. One memorable conversation took place soon after the news came through that G.K. Chesterton had died, so it must have been at the end of the summer term of 1936. I said how I had devoured as much Chesterton as I could lay my hands on as a schoolboy. Lewis warmed to the praise of Chesterton and I felt a new sympathy between us. I recall this now when I read how many of Lewis' affinities and friendships started from common interest in favorite books and writers.

One thing that occurs to me now, but which never struck me while Lewis was alive, is that I was rarely with him in the presence of others—except of course other students, for he gathered us together as undergraduates for what he called his "Beer and Beowulf" evenings, when we all sat on the floor in his room to declaim and translate Anglo-Saxon poetry. But my regular tutorials with him were individual tutorials, and when I renewed contact with him as a young writer, it was to have long conversations with him alone. On one of those occasions Hugo Dyson was present with us for dinner at Magdalen, but after the meal he departed. So I do not have those personal pictures of Lewis in company which enliven so many people's recollections of him. I did not get any clear impressions of Lewis' life outside the tutorial room and the lecture room. I recall only one occasion during my student days when Lewis spoke to me of his domestic situation. I asked him if he had been to see a certain play that had been performed in Oxford the previous day. He hadn't been able to, he said. "You see mother—I call her my mother though in fact she is not—insisted on my taking her to see that film of Anna Neagle as Victoria." It was insufferably tedious, he said, as films generally were, and he laughed scornfully about the way the camera focused for the emotional climax on glycerine tears rolling down the actress' face. At that time I felt it somewhat strange that a "mother" could so command the great scholar to the cinema, but later on it added to my insight into Lewis' faithfulness in humoring the whims of this very demanding woman. One might be tempted to feel anger at the way he gave himself to the tasks of washing dishes, mowing lawns, cleaning shoes, and other such chores, simply to help and please her. One is tempted to say, "What a waste of a man's valuable time" were it not that he accomplished so much as a writer anyhow that it would be difficult to conceive of his achieving more.

We students were all of course very much aware of Warnie. "The Colonel" my familiars called him, for no one could have failed more like a former military man. We thought him a great joke. He inhabited an inner study approached through Lewis' sitting room. There he could often be heard typing. But there was no one whose tutorial was not from time to time interrupted by a stealthy opening of the study door. The "Colonel" emerged, walked across the sitting room to the outer door with that kind of contrived "unobtrusiveness" that makes itself heavily obvious while the student's reading or the dialogue between student and tutor continued uninterruptedly. Having gone out, of course, the "Colonel" had to come back. The student waited in suspense until the performance was repeated in reverse. We could not in our ignorance and our innocence imagine why a bachelor don should saddle himself with a character whose regular processions across his tutorial room reminded us for all the world of Groucho Marx.

Until I was asked to contribute to this volume I have been reluctant to put pen to paper on the subject of Lewis. This is because Lewis was such a generous and unselfish man that most of my later connections with him arose out of, and centered upon, books which I had written. This puts me in a quandary (the sort of quandary that would have tickled Lewis hugely). It is a poor way to pay tribute to a great writer if I turn it into an occasion for talking about my own works. Yet it was my own work that brought about a renewal of meetings between us. It happened like this. In 1948-49 I wrote what was to be my first published book, *Repair the Ruins* (reflections on education from the Christian point of view), and I offered it to the publisher, Collins. They turned it down and their letter of rejection made it clear to me that it had been read by some professor of education, or someone of that kind. "I must try a publisher who is not in the educational field but who might send to a reader interested in theology," I said to myself, and promptly sent it off to Geoffrey Bles who at that time had a strong including such writers as Maritain and Berdyaev as well as s. Bles accepted the book and asked me to go and see him. it transpired that I was an ex-pupil of Lewis', Bles suggested we should try to interest him in the book. (His aim at this time was to try to get Lewis to introduce every new writer who came along—but that's another story.) Lewis very kindly agreed to look through the typescript. When he had done so, he asked me to go along for "dinner, bed and breakfast" at Magdalen so that he could take up some points with me before the book was sent to the printer.

When I wrote my next book, *English in Education*, Bles, to my surprise, got Lewis again to read it, and he did the same with my third typescript, *A Christian Philosophy of Education*, which in fact was never published. The only thing more astonishing to me now than Lewis' readiness to spend precious time and energy on my early typescripts was the way he turned my indebtedness to him into something for which I myself could be commended. "I think you are a very patient man," he wrote to me. "You might very well feel that you had been ready to put up with my comments for two years as an undergraduate, but not for a life-long critique." However, the critique, I'm glad to say, did continue. For in 1954 and 1955 I published my three allegorical novels which trace the visits of the narrator to a kind of purgatory, hell, and heaven. Out of sheer kindness Lewis wrote an encouraging letter to me as each book was published.

I have never kept a diary and I was lax in preserving letters—even Lewis'. I do not know on how many occasions I took advantage of his hospitality. "You know there is always dinner, bed and breakfast to be had here?" he ended a letter to me in 1954. In fact I went rarely, supposing that he must be over-plagued with visitors, and with ex-pupils especially. When I did go, it was to be taken along to the Senior Common Room for a sherry, and then to dinner in the college hall (if it was term-time) or in the Senior Common Room (if it was the vacation). After dinner the port and the madeir circulated in the Common Room and Lewis would whisper, advise against the madeira unless you've got a very strong hea We then repaired to his room to talk. During the course of ' evening he would boil a kettle of water on the floor and make Next morning he would knock on my door at 7:30 to take me ' walk in the grounds before breakfast. After breakfast we s^k

hands and parted, Lewis to get down to work promptly at nine o'clock.

Odd snippets of conversation linger in my mind from these occasions. I remember once, before Tolkien had published *The Lord of the Rings* and when he was little known as a writer, how we talked about *The Hobbit* and the way children took to it. "If you read it aloud, as I have done," I said, "there's only one false thing in the book, and it's that psychological stuff about the Took family at the beginning. It doesn't belong." Lewis was delighted to hear me say this. "How right you are," he said. "We all tried to get him to take it out. But he wouldn't." The remark conjures up an intriguing picture of Tolkien resisting the combined pressure of the Inklings.

I recall a visit I paid to Lewis shortly after the publication of my first theological novel, *The Devil's Hunting-Grounds*, in 1954. Perhaps I may repeat here something which I have recorded in my introduction to the reissue of the book. At the beginning of the story the narrator encounters his Guardian Angel who conducts him on a tour through localities in the hereafter where various heretics and half-believers go on indulging their misconceptions. The Guardian Angel is there to correct the earthbound notions of the narrator and other muddled characters. To suggest authoritativeness in modern terms I had made the angel, Lamiel, talk rather like a bureaucrat or a pedant. Why had I done this? Lewis asked me. "I thought it funny," I said. "It is, very funny indeed," Lewis grinned, but then went on to make a very serious point. Was I perhaps in danger of not treating angelhood seriously? This made me think. Especially since Lewis went on to say that when he first started to write *The Screwtape Letters*, he had intended to balance the correspondence between devils attacking the human soul with correspondence between angels protecting him. But when it came to the point and he tried to enter the angelic mind, he decided that the attempt was too presumptuous. Apparently had rushed in among the angels where Lewis had feared to ead.

When talk turned to Lewis' theological works, he revealed how ch hostile criticism had wounded him. "You don't know how I'm hated," he once said to me with feeling, adding as an afterthought, "loved too of course." No doubt envy and resentment were aroused in Oxford Senior Common Rooms by his popular success at the kind of polemical fisticuffs which donnish minds affected to despise. It has been said that Oxford dons objected to Lewis, not for becoming a Christian, but for advertising the fact. Unspoken rules of English decorum require one to be secretive about religious conviction. Lewis' way of putting intellectual and moral pressure on people in print for the purpose of converting them was an offence against academic etiquette. One must remember that Lewis had no degree in theology and was therefore, in the eyes of some, trespassing into other people's rightful terrain, an amateur taking on the experts. Professional academic theologians could obviously not be expected to enjoy having their thunder stolen. Lewis appealed to a vast audience over the heads of the university establishment and in defiance of academic protocol. In the eyes of some critics he was using a donnish know-how to mesmerize the innocent masses with dialectical conjuring tricks.

As Christians we know that Lewis was right to do what he did. The message of the gospels is unmistakable in this respect. The disciples were told to spread the gospel throughout the world, and there was no mention of their need to graduate in theology first. By comparison with what Lewis had to tell his generation, the protocol of even the most exalted university was trivial and petty. As for the resistance he sometimes encountered within the church itself, one can only assume that it was vengefully engineered by Screwtape. I say this while recalling an account he gave me of an encounter with some trendy clergymen at a gathering he had been invited to address. They did not conceal their coolness towards him.

No doubt this kind of hostility helped to drive Lewis into writing the Narnia books. He certainly regarded these stories as continuing the work begun in his apologetic. He spoke to me once as though he were turning away from one generation to address another. He implied that perhaps there wasn't much more he could do against the aridly unimaginative unbelief of our contemporaries, but that there was always hope in the young. He reacted warmly to appreciative talk of the Narnia books, and especially to any suggestion of a possible influence on children that might prove fruitful in later life. He could talk about the Narnia stories without self-consciousness. I remember one evening in his room how he dived down to the bottom of a bookshelf to dig out the French edition of *The Lion, the Witch, and the Wardrobe*. He was anxious to show me how the French artist had captured a totally different aspect of Aslan from that brought out in Pauline Baynes' drawings. He had nothing but praise for Pauline Baynes herself and for her illustrations. He thought them delightful. The lovableness of Aslan shone through her pictures. But the French artist had projected a more awesome, less cosy, indeed positively fearsome Aslan. The huggableness was gone. Here was a power you might well be advised to keep your distance from. Lewis' zest and pleasure in laying the book open before me to make the point stayed in my mind as such images sometimes do. It was a fit image of his own principle, that the Christian ought to be able to take the same delight—not greater, not less, not different—in his own good work as in someone else's. I suspect that the particular delight he took in praise of the Narnia books had something to do with the way their reception by readers and reviewers lifted him right out of the arena where the prophet and the preacher are sneered at and stoned.

I would not wish to make too much of the hostility to Lewis in academic theological circles. He had good friends in Oxford, high-powered theologians among them. I have two personal memories that illustrate this. On December 18, 1956, I took the train from Winchester to Oxford because I had been invited to have lunch with Eric Mascall at Christ Church. As I got off the train at Oxford, I came face to face with Lewis standing on the platform. He was ready to talk, but I could not linger because of my appointment to meet Mascall in Christ Church lodge. I explained this, and Lewis waved me off, saying, "Give my love to Eric." A memorable thing about these words is that I think they were the last I heard him say and the kind wave the last gesture I saw him make. When I returned home that evening I said to my wife, "I met Lewis on the station platform at Oxford, and I've never seen him look so utterly miserable. He looked tragic." Six days later he gave news of his marriage publicly in the *Times*. I was utterly bewildered. The image of Lewis' evident sadness and the news of the marriage did not fit together. Of course I assumed that he would no longer wish to be visited by ex-pupils. Only after a very long time did I come to understand that in the month of December 1956 Lewis had recently learned of Joy's fatal cancer and the decision to convert the civil marriage into a Christian marriage was being made.

Ten years later, in 1966, I was in Oxford one day for lunch with another distinguished theologian, Austin Farrer, then Warden of Keble College. Farrer and his wife, Katherine, gave me a graphic description of the remarkable occasion when Katherine felt that she simply must get in touch with Joy because something was wrong, and she called her by phone. At that very moment Joy had just collapsed on the floor, tripping over the telephone wire and bringing the telephone on to the floor beside her. As Katherine's call came through, she was able to reach the receiver and ask for help.

These two memories suggest to me that Eric Mascall and Austin Farrer, probably the two most distinguished Oxford theologians of their day, were among those Lewis had in mind when he made parenthetical deferential allusions to theologians more talented and more learned than himself. They figure several times among the speakers invited to address the Socratic Club. But of course Lewis was also surrounded by theologians of very different caliber—exponents of modernist heresies and subtly secularized uplift—and he was deeply aware that if he brought his readers into the fold only to leave them under the tutelage of such false teachers, he would not have served either God or them aright. So, for all his frontal attacks on atheism, he never ceased to adopt a strategy which allowed for a running battle on the side with the peddlers of soft-centered liberalism.

Lewis certainly enjoyed the fray. Especially he relished puncturing pretentiousness, whether it was the pretentiousness of a theologian who thought the time was ripe for remodelling the Christian faith to suit the temper of the age, or the pretentiousness of a bumptious student. When a too-solemn undergraduate propounded some highfalutin theory on the nature and function of imaginative literature, he would nod gravely and say, "Yes. Now how would you apply that to *The Tale of Peter Rabbit?*" There was more than a touch of the Irishman here—and in his polemical combativeness, his irony, and his rich imaginative power. The English media have lately managed to give a somewhat pejorative flavor to the term "Ulster Protestant" which has been exploited by detractors of Lewis. Even Tolkien, alas, spoke rather disparagingly of Lewis' regression to his native "Ulster Protestantism" in preference to the Roman Catholicism for which he had hoped to win him as convert. But in fact the Anglo-Catholic strain in Lewis' churchmanship (though he would certainly not have used the label for himself) was so foreign to "Ulster Protestantism" that he could not be categorized in those terms, as Tolkien must surely have known. Lewis was regular in his use of the confessional. And I have a personal memory that is relevant here. Once he and I were talking about "churchmanship." I said that I was attending a rather "spiky" Anglo-Catholic church and that sometimes there were things that cut against the grain with me. I mentioned the Good Friday liturgy in which the congregation file up to the altar rail and each in turn kisses the foot of a crucifix held by the priest. "I don't really go for that kind of thing," I said. Lewis turned on this immediately. "Oh but you *should*," he said. "The body must do its homage."

Now I suspect that, had I been expressing reservations about some converse evangelical, low-church, protestant (call it what you will) practice, he might well have turned on what I said with equal promptness. His habit in this respect was to defend what was under attack, to correct whatever prejudice might be emerging, by pressing the converse. This was an aspect of his tutorial technique carried over into conversation. And anyway, so anxious was he not to have his churchmanship docketed and labelled—either Evangelical or Anglo-Catholic—that he tended to run this way and that way across the dialectical seesaw to forestall its dipping down decisively at either end. For far more important to Lewis as a writer was the content of "mere Christianity" or "deep Christianity" whose intensity and coherence, over against the flabbiness and fragmentariness of contemporary theological liberalism, made intra-ecclesiastical variations of emphasis of less account in the immediate strategy of evangelism.

It is this emphasis in Lewis which has recently and rightly captured the imagination of both Roman Catholics and Protestant Evangelicals in the United States, who are combining in defence of the new trans-denominational orthodoxy against the secularistic dilution of creed and dogma that afflicts all denominations. They derive immense strength from C.S. Lewis. One might add that culture is on their side. The friendship between Lewis and Tolkien exemplifies the fact. Where there is theology that is great literature, or great literature that is theology, whether it be St. Augustine or Newman, John Bunyan or Lewis, you will find that the theology is never reductionist. Imaginative literature has naught for the comfort of liberal theologians. Those qualities of insight, imagination, intellectual sinew, and wholeness of grasp which make great writers are qualities which, when brought to bear in the theological field, conduce to the kind of credal firmness that both Lewis and Tolkien were blessed with.

It is interesting to recollect now how students looked on Lewis and Tolkien before either of them had made a name as a writer. Lewis was certainly the most popular lecturer in the English school in 1936 to 1938. When he was due to lecture, one of the largest halls had to be made available. This was simply because he was a lucid, entertaining, and highly instructive lecturer. From no other tutor's lectures could a student go away with notes so clear, orderly, and meaty. The series he called "Prolegomena to the Study of Mediaeval and Renaissance Literature" (lectures which he later put into book form as *The Discarded Image*) left us all with batches of clearly tabulated notes, for Lewis used the blackboard impressively and repeated important quotations at dictation speed. Small wonder that these lectures drew such enthusiastic audiences.

Tolkien, by the way, was a very different lecturer. His expertise lay in a specialism into which only the most linguistically oriented English students wished to venture very far. The custom in those days was for one's tutor to recommend his pupils to attend certain of the series of lectures announced in the term's schedule. I recall one term when Lewis recommended that we should go to Tolkien's lectures on "The Finn and Hengest Episode in Beowulf." This sounded rather abstruse. Moreover, the lectures were to be given twice, not once, a week. We were not at all sure that we wanted two hours per week on this topic even from the Professor of Anglo-Saxon. However, Lewis' recommendations were not lightly to be disregarded, and a friend and I went along to Tolkien's first lecture. We were surprised to find ourselves directed to one of the smallest lecture rooms and to discover an audience of little more than a dozen students (if my memory serves me well). The discourse was mostly beyond us. Tolkien littered the blackboard with etymologies, with Norse, Anglo-Saxon, and Sanskrit. But he was most evidently a likeable, unpretentious man whose only misjudgement was to think us capable of advancing in philological studies. So my friend and I decided to attend a couple more of the sessions before detaching ourselves from the course, having shown a decent degree of preliminary interest. Alas, by the second week the audience was down to about half a dozen. In such a small band we were only too noticeable as individuals. No doubt we were recognizably Lewis' pupils. Was it kind, let alone wise, to deplete the audience further? So we stuck it out to the end of the term. How absurd it seems now! Who would not think it a privilege to sit at Tolkien's feet for a few hours and listen to his voice, however abstruse its message?

Lewis, by contrast, seemed to be warmly in touch with his whole audience, giving them exactly what they wanted. The liveliness, the eloquence, the lucidity, and the unfailing good-humor he exuded were those of a man bursting with confidence and professionalism. Yet, if one arrived in good time for his lecture, before the previous hour's lectures were finished, and it was necessary to hang around outside the Examination Schools where the lectures took place, Lewis could be seen pacing up and down the pavement of the High Street, glancing frequently at his wristwatch, and looking outwardly as tense, nervous, and grave as if he were about to lecture in public for the first time. A few moments later he would be the unfaltering maestro on the rostrum. There was something about this contrast between tension and relaxation, gravity and cheerfulness, self-containment and over-flowing ebullience that is for me a powerful image of Lewis' character.

I am thinking of the personal burdens he shouldered, intensified as they were by Mrs. Moore's awkwardness and Warren's alcoholism, and how firmly they were prevented from saddening or souring any other aspects of his life. What an astonishing man he was at putting up with things! Childhood in Ireland, schooldays in England, war service in France were all marked at times by miseries which many a literary man would have turned into material for agonizing protest fiction. Yet how rarely is the note of grievance heard in Lewis' output! His own griefs and trials were mentioned only when mentioning them might help someone else to bear theirs.

I recall a curious little instance of this. After Lewis realized that the third book of my fictional trilogy, the vision of heaven, *Blessing Unbounded* (reissued as *Highway to Heaven*), had not attracted much notice from reviewers, he wrote a kind letter to me saying how much he himself had suffered when his early publications went unnoticed and unread. "Suffered" is not too strong a word, for he described graphically and feelingly what the aspiring writer goes through in this experience of grappling with early unsuccess—how the mind, reflecting on what is in store, tends by habit to move hopefully down familiar paths, and then has to be rudely checked and rebuffed, for those paths are now closed. This graphic description could have come only from someone who had felt his own disappointments keenly. But the record of it was unearthed only in order to sympathize helpfully with someone else.

For of course Lewis believed it a Christian duty to banish fruitless sadness. I recall how, in one of his more somber moods, he lamented to me the sad state of the church. "We're plagued with bad clergy," he said. "And it isn't just us. I'm told that the Roman Catholics have the same worry." I think this was said on the same occasion when he spoke more personally about the difficulty of prayer during dry periods. It was a time when there was, as always, plenty to worry about in public life and in the life of the church, if one were so minded; and I can hear Lewis now very sadly repeating, "*Deus absconditus*, indeed!" ("God is indeed the hidden God!") But what was surely most characteristic of Lewis was the way this mood suddenly gave place to another, which positively swept it aside. "You know the story of Saint Teresa?" he asked, and went on to describe her vision of our Lord standing on the opposite bank of a river and beckoning her to cross over to him. She stepped into the water and got into ever greater difficulties as the river got deeper and the current more dangerous. She was barely saved from being swept away, and turned, on reaching the further bank, to remonstrate with our Lord. "That's how I treat all my friends," he said. And Saint Teresa replied, "No wonder you get such rotten friends!" This sentence Lewis declaimed with relish and immediately swung into rocking laughter. "No wonder you get such rotten friends!"

I believe it is in *The Everlasting Man* that G.K. Chesterton remarks how he was drawn to Christ by the fact that people who praised him praised him for so many different reasons. Since Lewis himself said that we are all called to be "little Christs," it may not be inappropriate to note how richly varied are the accounts that have been given of him by those who knew him personally. Every account seems to enrich the portrait. It is clearly the portrait of a saint. Through all the accounts there runs the theme of Lewis' immense generosity in helping others. I am thinking not just of the numerous instances of often hidden financial charity and the renowned quickness to assist those he lived with in the arduous chores of daily life, but of the sheer magnitude of his achievement in answering the letters of those who sought his advice, in reading the manuscripts of people like myself whom he hastened to encourage, in guiding, criticizing, and stimulating so

C.S. Lewis / 19

many whose brains simply could not supply him—as could the brains of a Barfield or a Tolkien—with comparable counterstimulus.

For myself I am of course deeply aware of my indebtedness to Lewis, and yet—such was his character and his way of helping people—that I never say to myself now, "I ought to have troubled him less." On the contrary I find myself saying, "I wish I'd visited him more." Especially I regret that I did not go to see him after his wife's death. I regret too that I did not preserve all his letters to me. Those that survived I gave to the collection at the Bodleian Library. I thought I had given them all. But recently a postcard has turned up among my papers which was certainly my last message from Lewis. It is clearly a reply to a letter of mine saying that I should be in Oxford on a certain day and suggesting that I might call on him. The card is dated March 26, 1962. The note is handwritten:

The doctors hold out a hope of my being able to return to Cambridge on 24 April. If I do I shan't be here when you are. I'd v. much like a visit, however. Perhaps you'll be here some time in the vac? C.S.L.

I feel very sad now that I wasn't.

TWO

Paul Brand

by Philip Yancey

I FIRST MET Dr. Paul Brand on the grounds of the official U.S. Public
Health Service leprosarium in Carville, Louisiana. To get there,
I drove from New Orleans for two hours along the leveed banks of
the Mississippi River, past crumbling old plantations, crawfish
cafes, and gleaming new petrochemical factories. The Catholic
sisters who had drained swamps and built the hospital buildings a
hundred years before had deliberately located the leprosy center
away from major population centers. Laid out in a sprawling,
colonial style under huge oak trees, Carville resembled a movie set
of a Philippine plantation.

I knew of Dr. Brand's stature in the world medical community:
the offers to head up major medical centers, the distinguished
lectureships in Great Britain and America, the surgical procedures
named after him, the prestigious Albert Lasker award, his designa-
tion as Commander of the Order of the British Empire. But I waited
for him in a cubbyhole of an office hardly suggestive of such
renown. Stacks of medical journals, photographic slides, and
unanswered correspondence covered every square inch of an ugly

government-green metal desk. An antique window air conditioner throbbed at the decibel level of an unmuffled sports car. Charts of the labyrinthine government bureaucracy, not awards and citations, covered his office walls.

Finally, a slight man of less-than-average height entered the room. He had gray hair, bushy eyebrows, and a face that creased deeply when he smiled. In a British accent a striking contrast to the bayou accents heard in hospital corridors—he apologized for the flecks of blood on his lab coat, explaining that he had just been dissecting rabbit muscles.

That first visit with Dr. Brand lasted a week. We grabbed bits of conversations between management meetings, surgeries, clinical lectures, and animal research. I accompanied him on hospital rounds, leaving a wide berth in the hallways for the whirring electric wheelchairs and bicycles jerry-rigged with sidecars and extra wheels. I sat in the examination room as he studied the inflamed, ulcerated feet and hands of patients, trying to coax from them the cause of the injuries.

At night in his home, a rented wooden-frame bungalow on the grounds of the hospital, I would share an Indian-style meal with him and Mrs. Brand (also a doctor). Then Dr. Brand would prop up his bare feet (a trademark with him), and I would turn on the tape recorder for discussions that ranged from leprology and theology to world hunger and soil conservation.

In my role as editor of *Campus Life* magazine and writer for other magazines, I had interviewed many subjects over the years: rock music stars, successful business people, Pulitzer Prize winners, Olympic athletes. But something attracted me to Dr. Brand at a deeper level than I had felt with any other interview subject. I found in him a rich mixture of compassion, scientific precision, theological depth, and spiritual humility. In addition, his ideas on pain and pleasure were utterly different from any I had encountered in months of research.

My visit to Carville sparked a relationship that has grown and developed ever since. Later, when I left *Campus Life* to pursue freelance writing, I devoted the first five years to presenting the fruits of our dialogue: first in *Where Is God When It Hurts,* and then in two books we coauthored, *Fearfully and Wonderfully Made* and *In His Image.* I still maintain file folders labeled "Brand" stuffed with unused notes on topics we have never explored in print.

True friendship is measured, over time, by its effect on you. Has the association in some way changed your essential nature? As I compare the person I was in 1975, on our first meeting, and the person I am now, I realize that seismic changes have occurred within me, and Dr. Brand has been responsible for many of those tremors.

I was a college student during the 1960s. That tumultuous era awakened me to the ugly reality of poverty in the third world and here in American ghettos. Everything in America seemed to be cracking apart in those days: the Vietnam war chiseled away at our national ideals (and later Watergate proved the political cynics correct), revelations about pollution and the environment challenged the industrial ethic that had built our country, and the new counterculture exposed the hollow, image-conscious materialism that permeated business and the media. The issues are now so familiar as to become hackneyed. But to those of us who were forming a view of the world in that era, the sixties had a profound and permanent impact.

I recall my emotions in those years as being primarily anger, loneliness, and despair. I felt drawn toward books about the Holocaust, the Soviet Gulag, and other black holes of human history. I saw bright and talented friends give up on society and seek a different way through LSD and mescaline. Examining the church from such a jaded perspective, I noted mainly the hypocrisy of its members and their irrelevance to the world outside.

I now believe that God used Dr. Brand as one of his human agents to bring me out of that time with some stability. I was twenty-five when we first met; he was sixty. We made an odd pair, he with thinning gray hair and I with bushy hair in an Afro style. But somehow our friendship flourished. I look with deep appreciation on the privilege of learning from a great and humble man. I came to know him not through history, but as an actual living model, a man of God I could see in action—at Carville with his patients, in rural villages of India, as a husband and father, as a speaker at both medical and spiritual conferences. He, as much as anyone, has helped set my course in attitude, spirit, and ideals. In this tribute, I hope to identify partially how he has done so.

Dr. Brand achieved fame in the medical world mainly through his pioneering research on the disease leprosy. He had grown up in southern India, a child of missionary parents, and returned in 1946 after getting an education in England. During eighteen years in India he worked as a surgeon and teacher, directed the large Christian Medical College Hospital in Vellore, and founded a leprosy hospital known as Karigiri. Then, in 1965, he moved to the United States and began research work at the Carville hospital.

I did not expect to find gratitude as the chief characteristic of a man who had spent his life among victims of leprosy. Through the medical ignorance of others, those afflicted by leprosy are often isolated and reviled. In a place such as India, they are the outcasts of society, often doubly so as members of the untouchable caste.

Leprosy disproportionately afflicts the poor. Left untreated, its victims can develop the nerve damage and ulcers that eventually lead to facial disfigurement and loss of limbs. If anyone has a right to bitterness against the way the world is run, it should be someone who works with these unfortunates. And yet the single characteristic that most impressed me about Dr. Brand was his bedrock of gratitude.

For Paul Brand, gratitude began in childhood as simple appreciation of the natural world around him. He grew up in remote hill country, with none of civilization's normal barriers against nature. Snakes lived in the dark corners of the house and leopards stalked the forests outside, but apart from these dangers nature seemed wholly good. Until the age of nine he did his schoolwork sitting on a branch of a giant tamarind tree, dropping his completed assignments down to his mother on the ground below.

He spent childhood in a world of tropical fruit trees and of butterflies, insects, birds, and other animals. His artistic mother tried to capture its beauty visually, sometimes calling wildly to him to come and look at the sunset as she daubed watercolors on a canvas.

His father, a self-taught naturalist, saw nature as an awesome display of the genius of the Creator. He would lead his son to a towering four-foot termite mound and carefully expose the elaborate network of passages and their built-in cooling system, explaining the marvels of cooperative termite society. He would point to the sandy funnel of an ant lion trap, or the nest of a weaver bird, or a swarm of bees hanging from a tree.

The need for education interrupted Paul Brand's paradise, and he was sent to England at the age of nine. Five years later, as a fourteen-year-old student far from his native homeland, he received a cable that his father had died of blackwater fever. Two days after the cable, a letter from his father arrived, mailed by boat before his death. It described the hills around their home:

> Yesterday when I was riding over the windswept hilltops around Kulivalavu, I could not help thinking of an old hymn that begins, "Heaven above is deeper blue; flowers with purer beauty glow." When I am alone on these long rides, I love the sweet smelling wood, the dear brown earth, the lichen on the rocks, the heaps of dead brown leaves drifted like snow in the hollows. God means us to delight in his world. It isn't necessary to know botany or zoology or biology in order to enjoy the manifold life of nature. Just observe. And remember. And compare. And be always looking to God with thankfulness and worship for having placed you in such a delightful corner of the universe as the planet Earth.

Jesse Brand's son kept his advice, and keeps it to this day, whether hiking on the Olympic Peninsula or following birds around the swamps of Louisiana.

Another naturalist, the author Loren Eiseley, tells of an event he called the most significant learning experience of his long life. Caught on a beach in a sudden rainstorm, he sought shelter under a huge piece of driftwood. There, he found a tiny fox kitten, maybe ten weeks old. The kitten had no fear of humans. Within a few minutes it had engaged Eiseley in a playful game of tug-of-war, with Eiseley holding one end of a chicken bone in his mouth and the baby fox pulling on the other end.

The lesson he learned, said Eiseley, is that at the core of the universe, the face of God is a smile. Even the most ferocious animals—leopards and grizzlies and rhinoceroses—begin their lives playfully. Paul Brand, too, learned that lesson early. First in the hills of India, and later through a detailed study of the human body, he came to realize that at the heart of the natural world God could be found, and the God that he found was good.

Brand gained a sense of creatureliness, an awareness that he too had been willed into existence by a loving Creator and placed on a planet that, despite all its pain and fear, contained much beauty and goodness. He began to develop a consistent outlook of gratitude, undergirded by trust in the One who made the world.

My early conversations with Brand, coming as they did out of a time of personal searching, focused mainly on the dark spots and blemishes on the world. How could a truly good God allow such blemishes to exist? Dr. Brand took them on one by one. Disease? Did I know that 99 percent of all bacteria are healthful, not harmful? Plants could not produce oxygen and animals could not digest food without the assistance of bacteria. Most agents of disease, he explained, diverge from these necessary organisms only slight mutations.

What about birth defects? He went on to describe in detail the complex chemical changes that must work right to produce one healthy child. The great wonder is not that birth defects exist but that millions more do not occur. Could a mistake-proof world have been created so that DNA spirals would never err in transmission? No scientist could envision such a system without possibility of error in our world of physical laws.

Even at its worst, he continued, our natural world shows

evidence of careful design. Imagine a world without tornadoes or hurricanes, calamities that carry the damning label "acts of God." When hurricanes and monsoons do not come, the delicate balance of weather conditions gets upset, and killer droughts inevitably follow. How would you improve upon the world? he asked.

Brand's professsional life has centered on perhaps the most problematic aspect of creation, the existence of pain. He emphatically insists on pain's great value, holding up as proof the terrible results of leprosy—damaged face, blindness, and loss of fingers, toes and limbs—which nearly all occur as side-effects of painlessness. Leprosy destroys nerve endings that carry pain signals. People who do not feel pain almost inevitably damage themselves; infection sets in, and no pain signals alert them to tend to the wounded area.

"Thank God for pain!" Brand declares with the utmost sincerity. "I cannot think of a greater gift I could give my leprosy patients." (Actually, he tried to give them the protective gift, in a three-year research program to manufacture an artificial pain system.) Even in this instance, so commonly held up as a challenge to a loving God, he sees reason for profound gratitude.

The Bible records a dramatic scene when the overwhelming questions raised by the problem of pain were asked of God himself, in the Book of Job. The long speech God gave in reply has endured as one of the great nature passages in literature, a wonderful celebration of wildness as seen in mountain goats, ostriches, wild horses, snowstorms. But to the problem of pain God gave no direct answer, only this challenge to Job: if I, as Creator, have produced such a marvelous world as this, which you can plainly observe, cannot you trust me with those areas you cannot comprehend?

In that spirit, Dr. Brand learned at an early age that God wanted from him gratitude and trust—gratitude for those things he could see and appreciate, and trust regarding those things he could not. To his surprise, that attitude in him deepened even as he worked among people least likely to feel gratitude: the poorest of the poor, leprosy victims in India. In many of them, he saw the transformations that the love of God can produce. The immense human problems he lived among did not dissolve, but his faith supplied a confidence and trust that enabled him to serve God with gratitude and even joy.

Although I have great respect for Dr. Brand and his service to God, I also confess relief that he is not from the mold of St. Francis or Mother Teresa. I have immense respect for those rare individuals in history who have lived on a different plane, forsaking all material possessions, withdrawing from the world, and devoting themselves singlemindedly to a prophetic ideal. I learn much from them. And yet as I study their lives I sometimes have the nagging sense that they do not live in my world.

In his lifestyle, Dr. Brand has chosen the middle way of balancing off the material and the mystical, the prophetic and the pragmatic. At the hospital he left behind in Vellore, Brand is remembered for his spiritual depth and sacrificial service, but also for his practical jokes, love for marmalade and mangoes, and fast driving. As I emerged from the sixties, a decade never accused of possessing a sense of balance, I needed an example of someone who lived a well-rounded life in the midst of modern society, not off in a monastery or *ashram.* Dr. Brand had struggled with both extremes of the tensions facing modern civilization, while not giving in to either. On the one hand, he lived a "counterculture" lifestyle long before such a word entered American vocabulary. The Brand family eats simply, relying mainly on homemade breads and vegetables grown in their garden. Dr. Brand acknowledges a few reasons for discarding clothes—unpatchable rips, for instance—but lack of stylishness is certainly not one of them. Furniture in his home and office is, to put it kindly, unpretentious.

On the other hand, he has learned to use the tools made available by modern technology. Under his leadership, a hospital in the dusty backwater town of Vellore grew into the most modern and sophisticated facility in all of southwest Asia. Later, Brand came to the Carville hospital in the United States because it offered the technological support needed to research treatment procedures that would benefit millions of leprosy patients worldwide. And when personal computers were introduced in the 1980s, he signed up with boyish enthusiasm for one of the first IBMs, to assist his research and writing.

My conversations with Dr. Brand have often strayed to the question of lifestyle, for his experiences in India and America have afforded him a unique perspective on that issue. He has lived in one of the poorest countries and one of the richest. Affluence in the West, he recognizes, offers a deadly temptation. The enormous gap in economic development can create a moat separating the West from the rest of the world. Wealth can dull us to cries of need and justice, and too much comfort can sap the life from Christian work.

The lifelong tension over lifestyle traces back to Brand's childhood in India. After her husband's death, Paul's mother, Evelyn (Granny) Brand, took on the life of a "saint" in the traditional form. She lived on a pittance, devoting her life to reach villagers in five mountain ranges. She cared nothing for her personal appearance, not even allowing a mirror in her house. She continued hazardous journeys on her pony even after suffering concussions and fractures from falls. Although tropical diseases ravaged her body, she gave all her energies to treating the diseases and injuries of the people around her.

Sometimes Granny Brand would embarrass Paul with an intemperate outburst; at an official function in Vellore, for example, she might ask in horror, "How could you possibly dine on such fine food when I have people back in the hills starving to death this very night!" She died at age ninety-five among the people she loved, leaving Paul an unforgettable legacy. (The book *Granny Brand* tells her full story.)

From childhood Paul learned that Christian love is best applied person-to-person. His parents traveled from village to village, teaching health, sanitation, farming, and the Christian gospel. They left behind no lasting institutions, only their permanent imprint on thousands of lives. Singlehandedly, Granny Brand rid huge areas of a guinea worm infection that had persisted for centuries. Trusting villagers followed her instructions on building stone walls around their wells; no government program could have been so effective.

Yet Paul Brand himself found his most lasting successes through rigid scientific disciplines. At Vellore he fought his wife Margaret for space in the icebox, preserving cadaver hands to study by lamplight and practice surgical techniques. For years he puzzled over the physiology of leprosy: which cells does it attack, and why?

His most important medical discovery came when he observed that the leprosy bacillus did not destroy hands and feet but only attacked nerve tissue. Proving that theory required years of painstaking research. He had to keep track of patients and their injuries, searching whether all damage could indeed be traced to abuse of tissue, rather than the disease itself. The results of such research had a dramatic impact on the treatment of leprosy and other anesthetic diseases worldwide. Fifteen million victims of leprosy gained hope that, with proper care, they could preserve their toes and fingers and limbs. Damage was no longer inevitable.

Brand admits he would shed no tears if all advances from the industrial revolution onward suddenly disappeared—he prefers the simple village life in India, close to the outdoors. Yet unlike, say, Gandhi, he does not want to roll back modern civilization. He gratefully uses electron microscopes and thermograms and jet planes.

I sense in him a sort of "holy indifference" to many of the specifics that bother some sensitive Christians. He opposes waste in all forms. If an item is advertised as "disposable," he either refuses to buy it or else enjoys finding ways to make it last and last. He lives a remarkably disciplined and simple life. Yet, he says, "like the Apostle Paul, I have learned to be abased and to abound." To him technology, when used wisely and not destructively, offers a tool that helps advance the goals of the Kingdom.

A similar kind of balance characterizes other areas of Brand's life. His Christian faith developed through a combination of his parents' devout belief and his scientific training in medical school.

The church he attended in England, a member of the "Strict and Particular Baptist" denomination, had not adequately equipped him for intellectual challenges to his faith. But his missionary parents had demonstrated love in action, and although he found no quick answers, his faith remained intact as he deferred the questions to a later date, when he could approach them with more wisdom.

Originally, Brand had planned to go to India as a missionary builder, until an unlikely series of circumstances caused by World War II landed him in medical school. He traces much of his spiritual formation to the period of time just before medical school when he signed on for a year with an austere organization called the Missionary Training Colony. The Colony sought to equip missionaries for any rigorous situation they might encounter. It assigned students to live in crude huts, each of which accommodated twelve trainees. Brand's hut had hand-hewn furniture and a tiny charcoal stove which hardly sufficed in the British winter.

The Colony used a simple method of Bible training: each group of twelve trainees would work through the Bible in two years, wrestling with the issues they found there. No classes in theology and homiletics were held—Colony directors believed the Bible alone supplied all that was needed for theology and living. At regular intervals, the trainees would go out into cities and towns to conduct services, open-air meetings, and camp programs. Prewar Britain offered unusual opportunities for confrontational evangelism: sometimes Brand would find his open-air service sandwiched in between a communist rally and a meeting of black-shirt fascists.

Each summer the Colony also sent the groups of twelve "on trek" for a period of ten straight weeks, a program designed to teach teamwork and endurance. Brand's team loaded a two-wheel cart with clothes, tents, and all their necessary belongings. The boys harnessed themselves to the cart with long tow-ropes and marched along the backroads of Britain, singing as they went. When they reached a town in the afternoon, they would check with local church authorities for permission to conduct meetings in the church or in the town square. They slept in tents or on the floors of churches. In ten weeks, Brand's team covered 600 miles along the border of England and Wales.

Looking back, Dr. Brand fondly recalls that ten-week course as one of the great experiences of his life. It gave him a living, working example of the Body of Christ in action, with each member dependent on the others. Also, it taught him about his own cynicism, and about faith.

The Colony had one absolute rule for the trek: it must be conducted on faith. Each team began the trek with the equivalent of $100, sufficient to feed them for two or three days if no money or food came in. Otherwise, they depended entirely on what people gave to them, and they were never allowed to ask for gifts or take up a collection. The trek offered a chance for a sincere experiment in faith—for most of the boys at least.

Brand and two others viewed the faith rules of the Colony with considerable skepticism. The forced dependence seemed artificial to them—after all, they had relatives at home who could bail them out if necessary, so why starve for a principle? The three formed a secret club, each hiding away a few shillings. They made plans to sneak away from the group now and then to buy ice cream or a piece of cake.

After two or three such clandestine purchases, Brand and his friends realized they were wrong. The rest of the group was maturing into a deep sense of unity and faith, and the three knew their actions could poison that unity. They stopped their secret activities.

The next weeks offered Brand an unforgettable lesson in faith. After the stores and money supplies had run out, the twelve never knew whether they would have another meal. Yet supplies showed up, again and again, offered to them by villagers in astonishingly varied ways. They only missed one meal, a breakfast, but half an hour later a truck driver stopped beside them by the road and asked if they wanted some fresh melons. He had never done such a thing before.

Brand served as treasurer the last week of the trek, and after final expenses were paid, only three shillings and sixpence remained. As he went to the railroad station for final arrangements, one trunk suddenly turned up that had not been paid for. The price? Brand's jaw dropped open as the stationmaster quoted it: exactly three shillings and sixpence. The group of twelve headed back to the Colony, having never missed a meal, with no money but with a permanent lesson in faith.

The Colony taught Brand a lifelong pattern. He would use his own resources and intelligence as fully as possible but freely acknowledge dependence on God for the ultimate result. Later, in India, he had many opportunities to put faith into practice. The massive building plans at the Vellore hospital were all carried out with no sophisticated appeals for funds. Instead, the staff relied on simple prayer and belief. Brand also learned to seek wisdom from God during important research assignments, or in the midst of surgery. For him, faith became a daily habit that affected every part of his life. He no longer felt a dichotomy between the natural and spiritual realms.

During his time at the Missionary Training Colony, Paul Brand also gained a new perspective on the concept of "self-sacrifice." The Colony intentionally created difficult circumstances for its students in order to prepare them for conditions they might encounter in their mission assignments.

Primitive living conditions were not new to Brand. As a child, he had lived in a hand-built cabin with no water or electricity in a disease-infested region known as the "Mountains of Death." He had regularly fought off bouts of malaria. In bed at night he could hear rats crawling overhead. Yet when he arrived in England for schooling, he quickly saw that his own childhood had been far more adventurous and thrilling than the middle-class environment around him.

Gradually he learned an important part of his life philosophy: that pleasure and pain are not opposites, but rather mutually dependent parts of the richest experiences in life. Most often, the greatest pleasures come after great sacrifice, including considerable pain. The pattern holds true for musicians, who endure tedious hours of practice in order to produce great music, and for athletes, who willingly take on habitual pain in order to condition their bodies. Pleasure derived from producing great music and achieving athletic excellence can come in no other way except through pain.

Brand studied the life of the Apostle Paul, viewed the sufferings he endured in his attempts to preach the gospel as merely the cost required to fulfill his goals. Brand decided to stop looking at life as a polarity: avoid painful experiences, seek pleasurable ones. Rather, he would first ask, "Is this what God wants me to do?" If so, whatever came along, whether unpleasant or pleasant, provided an opportunity for him to exercise faith. He tried to think of normally unpleasant experiences as something of an adventure.

Brand's family went through trials that would horrify a modern mission executive. His first child was born while he was on wartime duty at a London hospital, fire-watching from the roof in order to dispatch emergency crews to deal with bombing victims. His second came while he was packing for India. He left his wife and children behind in England for six months while he established himself at Vellore (volatile political conditions in India delayed his wife from coming).

Missionary service in India took its own toll. As his body adjusted to a new climate, he broke out in prickly heat in the 110-degree temperatures and suffered through a series of tropical diseases. He practiced surgery under a homemade operating lamp hammered out of a sheet of aluminum.

In India, Dr. Brand insisted that each of his children (eventually six in all) be raised with the same freedom and sense of adventure he had known in childhood. Only half in jest, he calculated that it would be far better to have only four of his children live to adulthood than to have all six survive by living sheltered, overly protected lives. He encouraged them to climb, explore, and enjoy fully the adventures that India offered. As the children reached a certain age, the Brands had the wrenching experience of separation, as they sent each child off to England for high school.

Somehow, the family came through beautifully, and all six children survived.

The pattern I observed in Dr. Brand and his family reinforces a trend I have noted among various Christians I have interviewed for magazines. Not everyone fits the pattern, surely. But I have encountered it often enough that I can almost lump these interview subjects into two sets: Christian entertainers and Christian servants. The Christian entertainers—musicians, actors, speakers, comedians—fill our periodicals and television shows. We fawn over them, reward them with extravagant contracts and fan mail. They have everything they want, usually, including luxurious lifestyles. Yet many whom I've interviewed express to me deep longings and self-doubts.

In contrast, most of the Christian servants I have interviewed are not in the spotlight. People like the Brands toil unnoticed in remote parts of the country and the world. Relief workers, faithful pastors in communist lands, missionaries in the third world—these have all impressed me with a profound wisdom and deep-seated contentment strikingly absent from the entertainers. They work for low pay, long hours, no applause. They "waste" their talents and skills among the poor and uneducated. Yet in the very process of losing their lives, they find them. God reserves rewards for them which are unattainable in any other way.

Dr. Brand taught me that self-denial need not be viewed as an affliction, an opportunity for martyrdom. He adamantly refuses to look back on such experiences as sacrifice; they were, rather, challenges, tests of faith. They allowed an opportunity for God to redeem a hopeless situation.

At the hospital in Vellore he encountered seemingly insurmountable problems. Power failures and equipment breakdowns spoiled many of the research projects. He had to train unskilled Indian workers on the job. Attempts to treat leprosy patients ran into brick walls of opposition—initially, no one wanted them admitted to the main hospital.

Brand's theories on treatment and rehabilitation had to overcome centuries-old biases about the disease before they gained a foothold in the world medical community. Eventually, he had to find ways to provide new skills, housing, and employment for those leprosy victims who, even upon successful treatment and release, met hostility and rejection in their home villages. Yet, through it all, God's work was accomplished. Today, the leprosy facility at Karigiri, India, flourishes as a world-recognized training center, and its influence has spread to leprosy treatment centers across the earth.

A Christian ministry will require sacrifice—there are no exemptions. Human needs, whether social, spiritual, or physical, will guarantee that. But to a person committed to God, the very aspect of sacrifice can, paradoxically, become one of the most satisfying parts of service.

Dr. Brand expresses the guiding principle of his medical career this way: "The most precious possession any human being has is his spirit, his will to live, his sense of dignity, his personality. Once that has been lost, the opportunity for rehabilitation is lost. Though our profession may be a technical one, concerned with tendons, bones, and nerve endings, we must realize that it is the person behind them who is so important."

Although our conversations together cover a broad range of topics, inevitably they drift back to stories of individual human beings. The essentials of both his medical philosophy and theology had been worked out through constant contact with patients. Most often, these patients are the forgotten people, the poor and lonely who have been ostracized from family and village because of their illness. A medical staff can repair the marred facial features and fingers drawn into a claw-hand. They can provide that most basic human need: touch. But what can they do for the spirit of the patient, the corroded self-image?

It takes a few pennies a day to arrest leprosy's progress with sulfone drugs. But it takes thousands of dollars and the painstaking care of skilled professionals to restore to wholeness a patient in whom the disease has spread unchecked. In India, Dr. Brand began with hands, experimenting with tendon and muscle transfers until he found the very best combination to restore a full range of movement. The surgical procedures and rehabilitation stretched over months and sometimes years. He applied similar procedures to feet, correcting the deformities caused by years of walking without a sense of pain to guide the body in distributing weight and pressure.

New feet and hands gave a leprosy patient the capability to earn a living, but who would hire an employee bearing the scars of the dread disease? Brand's first patients returned to him in tears, asking that the effects of surgery be reversed so that they could get more sympathy as beggars. Then Dr. Brand and his wife saw the need to correct the cosmetic damage as well. They studied well-known techniques of surgery and modified them for the special problems of leprosy.

They learned to remake a human nose by entering it through the space between gum and upper lip (to utilize the moist lining inside) and fashioning a new nasal structure from transplanted bone. They learned to prevent blindness ov restoring the possibility of blinking: the paralyzed eyelid was attached to a muscle normally used for chewing. Margaret Brand worked daily with those patients, teaching them to make a chewing motion with their jaw every thirty seconds, in order to operate their eyelids and thus prevent dehydration of the eye.

Finally, they learned to replace lost eyebrows on the faces of their patients by tunneling a piece of scalp, intact with its nerve and blood supply, under the skin of the forehead and sewing it in place above the eyes. The first patients proudly let their new eyebrows grow to absurd lengths.

All this elaborate medical care went to "nobodies," victims of leprosy who most commonly made their living from begging. Many who arrived at the hospital barely looked human. Their shoulders slumped, they cringed when other people approached. Light had faded from their eyes. But months of compassionate treatment from the staff at Vellore could restore that light. For years people had shrunk away from them in terror; at Vellore, nurses and doctors would hold their hands and talk to them. They became human again.

In his twenty years in India, Dr. Brand operated on perhaps 3,000 hands and did thousands of other surgical procedures. He cannot possibly recall the details of each patient he contacted. But some stand out, such as John Kermagan, an irredeemable social misfit who learned of Jesus Christ through Granny Brand. It was the love shown by members of a local church that brought John back to health. He doubted whether any nonpatients would accept him, but they did, and thus helped transform his life.

Another patient named John showed up, a near-blind old man with severe damage from the disease. When he begged for surgery to free his stiff hands, Dr. Brand hesitated—many younger patients with a full life ahead of them were waiting in line for treatment. But the old man got his surgery. Although blind, he somehow learned to play the organ with insensitive fingers. He spent his last years as official organist at a mission leprosy sanatorium.

There were failures, of course, such as one man who threw himself in a well when he learned two fingers must be amputated. But over time the Brands learned that the human spirit, no matter how battered, can be reawakened and set free. Even in the most ugly, suspicious, hate-filled patients, the image of God began to shine through.

This lesson on the image of God is perhaps the greatest gift Dr. Brand has given me. The great societies of the West have been gradually moving away from an underlying belief in the value of a single human soul. We tend to view history in terms of groups of people: classes, political parties, races, sociological groupings. We apply labels to each other, and explain behavior and ascribe worth on the basis of those labels. After prolonged exposure to Dr. Brand, I realized that I had been seeing large human problems in a mathematical model: percentages of Gross National Product, average annual income, mortality rate, doctors-per-thousand of population. I had been wrestling with "issues" facing "humanity." I had not, however, learned to love individuals—people created in the image of God.

I would not predict a leprosarium in India as the most likely place to learn about the infinite worth of human beings, but a visit there makes the lesson unavoidable. The love of God is not mathematical; we cannot precisely calculate the greatest possible good to be applied equally to the world's "poor and needy." We can only seek out a person, and then another, and then another, as objects for Christian love.

Gratitude. Balance. Sacrifice. The Image of God. In no way have I mastered these principles that Dr. Brand has demonstrated for me. I must remind myself of them every day. When I look outside my window in downtown Chicago I ask myself again, How can I be grateful in view of such human misery everywhere? How can I achieve a sense of balance in a world tilting toward chaos? Why should I worry about sacrifice or self-denial when my culture offers me an easier, more pleasurable way? And how can one individual matter? I ask these questions, and perhaps I always will.

But as I ask them, I also give thanks that I have had Dr. Brand to help lead me on the way to answers. He would not want me to imply that these qualities have arisen from his own person. The same Holy Spirit that motivated his mother and father in India, and now animates him, is the One who wants to bring adventure and love of life to all who are willing to lose themselves in him. I hope that our collaboration in writing has made it possible for other persons to see those same principles and that same Spirit at work in Paul Brand.

THREE

William Wilberforce

by Charles Colson

S EVERAL HUNDRED MILES OFF THE COAST OF AFRICA, 1787. The
scudding clouds obscured the moon as the heavy schooner
pitched forward in the dark waters. The decks were empty save for
the lone sailor on the late watch and a cluster of others at the wheel.

The rest of the crew tossed fitfully in their hammocks; in the
main cabin a fat tallow candle burned low, flickering in the
tropical air. The captain, a balding man with thick sideburns,
squinted as he dipped his quill in a well of sepia ink and continued
his log report, laboriously noting progress on their voyage to
Jamaica. The flogging that day of the cabin boy was the only
incident of note.

In the dark hold below, the heavy air was almost palpable with
the stench of human waste and vomit. Five hundred and twelve
black men and women lay on their sides in the filth, crammed so
tightly together that the chest of each was pressed against the
sweaty back of his neighbor, their legs drawn up, their feet on the
heads of those in the next anguished row.

Moans, sobs, and feverish delirium combined with the creaks of the ship's aged timbers to transform the putrid hold into a scene from hell.

And for the slaves, it was. They were captured Africans, some the prisoners of tribal wars or petty criminals, others the unsuspecting dinner guests of visiting Englishmen. But all had been rounded up, chained and held in a stockade, then sold to the highest bidder who had come into port.

The elderly and unfit had been dispatched with a pistol shot or clubbed to death, their bodies dragged into the shallows, where they bobbed gently until caught in the flow of the tide.

Others were branded, then whipped and shoved into small boats to be ferried to the large oceangoing vessels laying at anchor offshore. Weeping, screaming for mercy, they were hoisted onto the tall ship and forced into the stinking hold, then shackled into irons.

But not all were immediately driven below. The crew, though diseased and ill-treated themselves, claimed the one sordid privilege of their trade—the pick of the slave women. Once off the coast, the ship became half bedlam, half brothel, as one captain put it.

Now on this cloudy night, several weeks into the voyage, sixty slaves were already dead. Some had succumbed to the fevers raging through the rotten hold. Others, driven insane by the horrors, were disposed of by the crew. Each morning as the lower decks were opened, the dead and the near-dead were removed, their bodies thrown overboard to the waiting sharks.

Whenever the captain watched this morning ritual, he cursed as each black body hit the choppy water, muttering as he calculated his lost profits. Certainly he had no legal worries, however, about throwing sick slaves to their deaths: in a celebrated case in England's high court only four years earlier, slaves had been described as "goods and chattels," the chief justice observing that it was "exactly as if horses had been thrown overboard." And in the colonies, the word of a black could not be taken over a white. That was the law.

At any rate, no slave remaining in the dark hold of that slave ship had any idea what was in store if he did survive the three-month journey: he would be auctioned naked in the marketplace, then—if he survived the treatment of his new master—life would be merely a dogged hold on survival in the cane fields. He would never know or see in his short lifespan the nation which would so richly profit from his misery: England.

London, 1787. In the city described as "one vast casino," the rich counted their profits from the slave trade while in a fog of claret. They lost and rewon their fortunes over gaming tables in prestigious private clubs; duels were the order of the day to preserve honor.

Corruption in government was so widespread that very few members of parliament thought twice about the usual practice of buying votes. And since the slave trade was not only considered successful business, but a national policy, political alliances revolved around commitment to the trade. It became euphemistically known as "the institution," the "pillar and support of British plantation industry in the West Indies."

The planters and gentlemen who grew rich through the profits of their trade investments became an increasingly powerful force in parliament, paying £3,000 to £5,000 to "buy" boroughs, which sent their representatives to the House of Commons; hence the term "rotten boroughs." Their influence grew until a large bloc of the House was controlled by the vested influence of the slave traders.

The same attitude reigned in the House of Lords. After all, the horrors of the trade were far away and unseen. But the returns on their investment were often 100 percent; the cotton and sugar and profits the slaves provided were very tangible. If the slave trade made England stronger—and the rich richer—it could not be a bad thing.

So they counted their returns and, when time weighed heavy on their hands, turned to whatever distraction took their fancy. The town's theaters were surrounded by clusters of brothels; hordes of prostitutes (estimated at one out of every four women in the city) specialized in any manner of perversion for those whose appetites had grown jaded.

High society similarly revolved around romantic intrigue and adulterous affairs. An upper class couple might not see one another in public for weeks during the social season; no self-respecting hostess would have such poor taste as to invite a husband and wife to the same social event.

The poor had no such opportunity to escape from one another. Crammed together in grimy cobblestoned neighborhoods, they sweated out a living as cogs in Britain's emerging industrial machines. Pale children worked as many as eighteen hours a day in the cotton mills or coal mines, bringing home a few shillings a month to their parents, who often spent it on cheap gin. One-eighth of the deaths in London were attributed to excessive drinking.

Highwaymen were folk heroes; Newgate and other infamous prisons overflowed with debtors, murderers, children, and rapists. A twelve-year-old thief might be hung the same day as a celebrated robber, with huge crowds relishing the expiration of the celebrity while scarcely noticing the life choking out of the other.

Frequent executions provided one form of public amusement, bull baiting another. Bulls were tortured with fire or acid to keep them lively; if the attacking dogs failed to be gored, their throats would be slashed to satisfy the crowd's thirst for blood. At county fairs, badgers, their tails nailed to the ground, were worried to death by dogs; sheep were slaughtered as savagely as possible for popular sport.

At one such event, the Duke of Bedford and a Lord Barrymore staged a bet in which the latter, for £500, brought forth a man who ate a live cat before a cheering crowd.

In short, London was the center of a country where unchecked human passions had run their course. Few were the voices raised in opposition.

#4 OLD PALACE YARD, LONDON, OCTOBER 25, 1787. It was still dark when the slight young man pulled the dressing gown around his small, thin frame and sat at the oak desk in the second floor library. As he adjusted the flame of his lamp, the warm light shone on his piercing blue eyes, oversized nose, and high wrinkling forehead—an agile face that reflected the turmoil of his thoughts as he eyed the jumble of pamphlets on the cluttered desk. They were all on the same subject—the horrors of the slave trade.

He ran his hand through his wavy hair and opened his well-worn Bible. He would begin this day, as was his custom, with a time of personal prayer and scripture reading. But his thoughts kept returning to the pamphlets' grisly accounts of human flesh being sold, like so much cattle, for the profit of his countrymen. He couldn't wipe the scenes from his mind. Something inside him— that insistent conviction he'd felt before—was telling him that all that had happened in his life had been for a purpose, preparing him to meet that barbaric evil head-on.

William Wilberforce was born in Hull in 1759, the only son of a prosperous merchant family. Though an average student at Cambridge, his quick wit made him a favorite among his fellows, including William Pitt, who shared his interest in politics. Often the two young men spent their evenings in the gallery of the House of Commons, watching the heated debates over the American war.

After graduation, Wilberforce ran as a conservative for a seat in parliament from his home county of Hull. He was only twenty-one—but the prominence of his family, his speaking ability, and a generous feast he sponsored for voters on election day carried the contest.

When he arrived in London, the city's elegant private clubs and societies welcomed him; Wilberforce soon fell in step, happily concentrating on the pursuit of pleasure and political advancement.

He spent his evenings with friends, consuming enormous dinners accompanied by multiple bottles of wine and then perhaps a play, dancing, or a night of gambling. His friendship with William Pitt and other young politicians flourished; then, in early 1784 Pitt, though only twenty-four, was elected prime minister. Inspired, Wilberforce took a big political gamble, surrendering his safe seat in Hull to stand for election in Yorkshire, the largest and most influential constituency in the country.

It was a grueling campaign, the outcome uncertain until the closing day, when Wilberforce addressed a large rally. James Boswell, Samuel Johnson's celebrated biographer, stood in the cold rain and watched Wilberforce, barely over five feet tall, prepare to address the wet, bored crowd.

"I saw what seemed a mere shrimp mount upon the table," Boswell wrote later, "but as I listened, he grew and grew, until the shrimp became a whale."

Such was the power of the young parliamentarian's oratory; he was elected from Yorkshire. As an intimate of the prime minister, respected by both political parties, William Wilberforce seemed destined for power and prominence.

After the election, Wilberforce's mother invited him to join his sister and several cousins on a tour of the Continent. Wilberforce agreed, then ran into his old schoolmaster from Hull, Isaac Milner, and spontaneously asked him to join the traveling party.

That vacation was to change Wilberforce's life.

Isaac Milner was a stocky, big-boned man with a mind as robust as his body. He was eager to debate the quick young orator, though he could not match his skill. As their carriage ran over the rutted roads between Nice and the Swiss Alps, their lively discussion turned to religion. Wilberforce, who considered his flirtation with Methodists—as the religious enthusiasts of his day were known—a childish excess, treated the subject flippantly. Milner growled at his derisive wit, stared moodily out the carriage window, and declared, "I am no match for you . . . but if you really want to discuss these subjects seriously, I will gladly enter on them with you."

Provoked by the older man's remark, Wilberforce entered in, eventually agreeing to read the scriptures daily.

As the summer session of parliament got underway, Wilberforce returned to the whirl of the London social scene. But his diary reveals subtle changes in his tastes. One party, of the kind he routinely attended, was now described as "indecent"; his letters began to show concern for corruptions he had scarcely noticed before. The seeds of change had been planted.

That fall of 1785, as he and Milner returned to the Continent to continue their tour, Wilberforce was no longer frivolous. He pressed his companion about the scriptures. The rest of the party complained about their preoccupation as they studied a Greek New Testament on their coach between cities.

Wilberforce returned to London in early November 1785 faced with a decision he could no longer avoid. He knew the choice before him: on one hand his own ambition, his friends, his achievements; on the other a clear call from Jesus Christ.

Selections from his diary show the Holy Spirit's relentless pursuit:

Nov. 27: I must awake to my dangerous state, and never be at rest till I have made my peace with God. My heart is so hard, my blindness so great, that I cannot get a due hatred of sin, though I see I am all corrupt, and blinded to the perception of spiritual things.

Nov. 28: Lord, I am wretched, and miserable, and blind, and naked. What infinite love, that Christ should die to save such a sinner, and how necessary is it He should save us altogether, that we may appear before God with nothing of our own!

Nov. 29: Pride is my greatest stumbling block . . .

Nov. 30: Was very fervent in prayer this morning, and thought these warm impressions would never go off. Yet in vain endeavor in the evening to rouse myself. . . . What can so strongly show the stony heart? O God, give me a heart of flesh! . . .

On December 2, weary and in need of counsel, Wilberforce resolved to seek out a spiritual guide. He made a fascinating but unlikely choice: John Newton.

Son of a sailor, Newton had gone to sea at age eleven, where he eventually deserted, was flogged, and exchanged to a slave ship.

Later Newton himself became a slave on an island off the coast of Africa. Rescued by his father, he sailed on a slave ship and in 1750 was given command of his own slaver. Then, on a passage to the West Indies, Newton was converted to Jesus Christ, later expressing his wonder at the gift of salvation to "a wretch like me" in his famous hymn, "Amazing Grace."

Newton was subsequently ordained in the Church of England; his outspoken singlemindedness in spiritual matters must have attracted a buffetted Wilberforce.

Though he cautioned Newton in a note to "remember that I must be in secret . . . the face of a member of parliament is pretty well known," he called on the old preacher. Newton reassured him and, prophetically, told Wilberforce to follow Christ but not to abandon public office: "The Lord has raised you up to the good of His church and for the good of the nation."

Wilberforce knew he had to share his new faith with his old friends. The responses were predictable: some thought his mind had snapped under the pressures of work; many were convinced his new-found belief would require him to retreat from public life. Still others were simply bewildered: how could a well-bred and educated young man, with so much promise, get caught up in the religious exuberance of Methodism, a sect appealing only to the common masses?

The reaction Wilberforce cared about most was Pitt's. He wrote to the prime minister, telling him that though he would remain his faithful friend, he could "no more be so much of a party man as before."

Pitt's understanding reply revealed the depth of their friendship; but after their first face-to-face discussion, Wilberforce wrote in his diary: "He tried to reason me out of my convictions but soon found himself unable to combat their correctness, if Christianity was true. The fact is, he was so absorbed in politics, that he had never given himself time for due reflection on religion."

Though Pitt and Wilberforce were to continue as friends and allies, their relationship would never again be the same. And, indeed, one of the great sorrows of Wilberforce's life was that the friend he cared for most never accepted the God he loved more.

On this foggy Sunday morning in 1787, as Wilberforce sat at his desk, he reflected that even if Pitt did not share his commitment to Christ, God had brought him brothers who did. He thought about Thomas Clarkson, the red-headed clergyman and brilliant essayist who had visited so often that year while Wilberforce had been ill—Clarkson, whose passion for justice and righteousness awed him.

These were Clarkson's pamphlets strewn across his desk, shocking papers detailing the brutality of the slave trade. Wilberforce had been poring over them for months. He stared out the window at the gray English drizzle, but all he could see were burdened slave ships leaving the sun-baked coasts of Africa.

Then, on the cobblestone street below, two cloaked figures stumbled into view, leaning heavily on one another. Their raucous voices jangled together in a few bars of a lewd song as they lurched toward home, near collapse after a long night of carousing. Such a common sight in London.

He turned back to the desk and the journal filled with tiny, cramped writing meant for no one's eyes but his own. He thought about his conversion—had God saved him only for the eternal rescue of his own soul, or also to bring his light to the world around him? He could not be content with the comfort of life at Palace Yard, the stimulating debates in parliament. . . . True Christianity must go deeper. It must not only save but serve; it must bring God's compassion to the oppressed, as well as oppose the oppressors.

His mind clicked, and he dipped his pen in the inkwell. "Almighty God has set before me two great objectives," he wrote, his heart suddenly pumping with passion, "the abolition of the slave trade and the reformation of manners."

With those words, the offensive was launched for one of the epic struggles of modern history. God's man, called to stand against the entrenched evils of his day: the self-indulgent hedonism of a society pockmarked by decadence and the trade which underwrote those excesses, the barbaric practice of trafficking human flesh for private gain.

From his discussions with Thomas Clarkson and others, Wilberforce knew the issue had to be faced head-on in parliament. "As soon as ever I had arrived thus far in my investigation of the slave trade," he wrote, "so enormous, so dreadful, so irremediable did its wickedness appear that my own mind was completely made up for the abolition. A trade founded in iniquity and carried on as this was, must be abolished, let the policy be what it might."

Thus, throughout the wet fall of 1787 he worked late into the nights, joined by others who saw in the young politician the man God had raised up to champion their cause in parliament.

There was Granville Sharpe, a hook-nosed attorney with a keen mind. He was already well-known for his successful court case making slavery illegal in England herself—ironic in a time when her economic strength depended on slavery abroad.

Zachary Macaulay, a silent, patient researcher, sifted through extraordinary stacks of evidence, organizing facts to build damning indictments against the slave trade. A dedicated worker who regularly took pen in hand at four o'clock every morning, he became a walking encyclopedia for the rest of the abolitionists; whenever Wilberforce needed information, he would look for his quiet, heavy-browed friend, saying, "Let us look it up in Macaulay!"

Thomas Clarkson, of course, was Wilberforce's right hand and scout, conducting various exhausting—and dangerous—trips to the African coast. He once needed some evidence from a particular sailor he knew by sight, though not by name. He searched through dozens of slave vessels in port after port, until finally, after searching 317 ships, he found his man.

Suddenly, in February of 1788, while working with these friends and others, Wilberforce fell gravely ill. Doctors warned he could not last more than two weeks; in Yorkshire the opposition party, cheered by such news, made plans to regain his seat in parliament.

By March he was somewhat better, though not well enough to return to parliament. He asked Pitt to introduce the issue of abolition in the House for him. Purely out of the warmth of their friendship, the prime minister agreed.

So in May of 1788, Pitt, lacking Wilberforce's passion but faithfully citing his facts, moved a resolution binding the House to discuss the slave trade in the next session.

His motion provoked a lukewarm debate, followed by a vote to duly consider the matter: those with interest in the trade were not worried about a mere motion to *discuss* abolition. Then Sir William Dolben, a friend of Wilberforce's, introduced a one-year experimental bill to regulate the number of slaves that could be transported per ship; after several MPs visited a slave ship lying in a London port, the debates grew heated, with cries for reform.

Now sensing the threat, the West Indian bloc rose in opposition. Tales of cruelty in the slave trade were mere fictions, they said; it was the happiest day of an African's life when he was shipped away from the barbarities of his homeland. The proposed measure, added Lord Penrhyn hysterically, would abolish the trade upon which "two thirds of the commerce of this country depended."

In response to such obstinate claims, Pitt himself grew passionate. Threatening to resign unless the bill was carried, he pushed Dolben's regulation through both Houses in June of 1788.

The success of Dolben's bill awakened the trade to the possibility of real danger. By the time a recovered Wilberforce returned to the scene, they were furious and ready to fight, shocked that Christian politicians had the audacity to press for religiously based reforms in the political realm. "Humanity is a private feeling, not a public principle to act upon," sniffed the Earl of Abingdon. Lord Melbourne angrily agreed: "Things have come to a pretty pass when religion is allowed to invade private life."

Wilberforce and the band of abolitionists knew that privatized faith, faith without action, meant nothing at all if they truly followed the God who mandated justice for the oppressed.

Wilberforce's first parliamentary speech for abolition on May 12, 1789, shows the passion of his convictions, as well as his characteristic humility:

> When I consider the magnitude of the subject which I am to bring before the House—a subject, in which the interests, not of this country, nor of Europe alone, but of the whole world, and of posterity, are involved... it is impossible for me not to feel both terrified and concerned at my own inadequacy to such a task. But ... I march forward with a firmer step in the full assurance that my cause will bear me out ... the total abolition of the slave trade ...
>
> I mean not to accuse anyone, but to take the shame upon myself, in common, indeed, with the whole Parliament of Great Britain, for having suffered this horrid trade to be carried on under their authority. We are all guilty—we ought all to plead guilty, and not to exculpate ourselves by throwing the blame on others.

But the passionate advocacy of Wilberforce, Pitt, and others was not sufficient to deter the interests of commerce in the 1789 session. The West Indian traders and businessmen pressured the House of Commons, which voted not to decide.

The House's vote to postpone action spurred Wilberforce to gather exhaustive research. He and his coworkers spent nine and ten hours a day reading and abridging evidence; in early 1791 he again filled the House of Commons with his thundering yet sensitive eloquence.

> Never, never will we desist till we have wiped away this scandal from the Christian name, released ourselves from the load of guilt under which we at present labour, and extinguish every trace of this bloody traffic, of which our posterity, looking back to the history of these enlightened times, will scarce believe that it has been suffered to exist so long a disgrace and dishonour to this country.

However, the slave traders were equally determined. One member argued:

Abolition would instantly annihilate a trade, which annually employed upwards of 5,500 sailors, upwards of 160 ships, and whose exports amount to 800,000 sterling; and would undoubtedly bring the West India trade to decay, whose exports and imports amount to upwards of 6,000,000 sterling, and which give employment in unwards of 160,000 tons of additional shipping, and sailors in proportion.

He paused, dramatically, and pointed up to the gallery, where a number of his slave-trading constituents watched approvingly, exclaiming brazenly, "These are my masters!"

Another member, citing the positive aspects of the trade, drew a chilling comparison: the slave trade "was not an amiable trade," he admitted, "but neither was the trade of a butcher . . . and yet a mutton chop was, nevertheless, a very good thing."

Incensed, Wilberforce and other abolitionists fought a bitter two-day battle; members shouted and harangued at one another, as spectators and press watched the fray. By the time the votes were cast, in the terse summation of one observer, "Commerce clinked its purse," and Wilberforce and his friends were again defeated.

After their loss in 1791, Wilberforce and his growing circle of Christian colleagues, grieved and angered by the unconscionable complacency of parliament, met to consider their strategy.

They were a varied group, marked by the common devotion to Christ and to one another. In addition to Wilberforce, the lawyer Sharpe, and researchers Clarkson and Macaulay, there was James Stephen, a handsome West Indian who had witnessed the evils of the slave trade firsthand. Stephen's passion for abolition could burst into fiery anger against those who propagated such evil; occasionally, in later years, he would even burst forth at Wilberforce when frustrated by the course of their battle.

Thomas Gisborne, a close friend of Wilberforce's at Cambridge, had lost touch with him after leaving college. Now a clergyman and gifted orator, Gisborne wrote to Wilberforce, asking to join with him in the movement.

Henry Thornton, a member of parliament, was a calm, wealthy banker who brought managerial ability to the diverse group. He also became one of Wilberforce's closest friends, ready to weather any political storms or disappointments that might lie ahead.

These men, along with Thomas Babington, Charles Grant, and writer Hannah More were just a few of the personalities who gathered together to fight the slave trade. Committed to Christ as Lord above all, they began to form a bond based on more than the allegiance of a united political cause. They were, says one historian, "a unique phenomenon—this brotherhood of Christian politicians. There has never been anything like it since in British public life."

In 1792, as it became apparent that the fight for abolition would be long, Henry Thornton suggested to Wilberforce that they gather together at his home in Clapham, a village four miles south of Westminster, convenient to parliament yet set apart.

Thornton had thought out his plan and believed that living and worshiping together would draw the brotherhood closer to God and to one another. His home, "Battersea Rise," was a lively Queen Anne house on the grassy Clapham Common; as friends came to live or visit, Thornton added extra wings. Eventually Battersea Rise had thirty-four bedrooms, as well as a large, airy library designed by Prime Minister Pitt.

This oval, bookcase-lined room was the site of many an intense prayer meeting and late-night discussion. Here, in the heart of the house, Thomas Clarkson related the horrors he had witnessed on his fact-finding missions to the African coast; here Henry Thornton led in prayer as all knelt on the polished floor. Here they met in hours-long "cabinet councils," as they prepared for their parliamentary battles.

Wilberforce moved to Clapham to take up part-time residence in Thornton's home; then, after his marriage in 1797, he moved to Broomfield, a smaller house on the same property.

Clapham was also a place where the brothers sharpened and

reproved one another. At several points the fiery James Stephen detailed several of Wilberforce's faults to him; to each such criticism Wilberforce replied, "Go on, my dear sir, and welcome. . . . Openness is the only foundation and preservative of friendship."

Such was Wilberforce's character—he welcomed not only the rebukes of his brothers, earnestly committing his failures to God, but he also brimmed over with the vitality which characterizes great saints.

In later years, this was often manifest in his attitudes toward his children and those of his colleagues. Sometimes he was "as restless and volatile as a child himself," Henry Thornton's eldest daughter, Marianne, recalled. "During the long and grave discussions that went on between him and my father and others he was most thankful to refresh himself by throwing a ball or a bunch of flowers at me, or . . . going off with me for a race on the lawn. . . . One of my first lessons was I must never disturb papa when he was talking or reading, but no such prohibition existed with Mr. Wilberforce."

Such was life at Clapham: a deeply committed and joyful community of Christian families, living in harmony as they pursued the great calls God had issued them: both the abolition of the slave trade and the reformation of a decadent society around them.

As the Clapham community analyzed their battle in 1792, they were painfully aware that many of their colleagues in parliament were puppets—unable or unwilling to stand against the powerful economic forces of their day.

So Wilberforce and his workers went to the people. In 1792 Wilberforce wrote, "It is on the general impression and feeling of the nation we must rely . . . so let the flame be fanned."

The abolitionists distributed thousands of pamphlets detailing the evils of slavery, spoke at public meetings, circulated petitions. The celebrated poet William Cowper had written "The Negro's Complaint," a poem that was set to music and sung in many a fashionable drawing room; Josiah Wedgwood designed a cameo— which became the equivalent of a modern-day campaign button—

of a black man kneeling in bondage, whispering the plea that was to become famous: "Am I not a man and a brother?"

They organized a boycott of slave-grown sugar, a tactic even Wilberforce thought could not work, but which gained a surprising following of some 300,000 across England.

Later in 1792, incredibly, Wilberforce was able to bring 519 petitions for the total abolition of the slave trade, signed by thousands of British subjects, to the House of Commons. As their movement rode on a surging tide of public popularity, Wilberforce's usual impassioned eloquence on the subject profoundly disturbed the House.

In the year 1788 in a ship in this trade, 650 persons were on board, out of whom 155 died. In another, 405 were on board, out of whom were lost 200. In another there were on board 402, out of whom 73 died. When captain Wilson was asked the causes of this mortality, he replied, that the slaves had a fixed melancholy and dejection; that they wished to die; that they refused all sustenance, till they were beaten in order to compel them to eat; and that when they had been so beaten, they looked in the faces of the whites, and said, piteously, "Soon we shall be no more."

Even the vested economic interests of the West Indian bloc could not gloss over these appalling facts or ignore the public support the abolitionists had gained. But again the slavers exercised their political muscle. The House moved that Wilberforce's motion should be qualified by the word "gradually" and it was thus carried. The slave traders had no real fear of a bill which could be indefinitely postponed by that simple yet powerful word.

Though Wilberforce was wounded at yet another defeat, he had a glimmer of new hope. For the first time the House had voted for an abolition motion; with the force of the people behind the cause, it would only be a matter of time.

Suddenly, the events of the day reversed that hope. Across the English Channel the fall of the Bastille in 1789 had heralded the people's revolution in France. By 1792 all idealism vanished; the September Massacres had loosed a tide of bloodshed in which the mob and the guillotine ruled France.

In England, fear of similar revolution abounded; any type of public agitation for reform was suspiciously labeled as "Jacobinic," after the extreme revolutionaries who fueled France's Reign of Terror. This association, and ill-timed slave revolts in the West Indies, effectively turned back the tide of public activism for abolition.

The House of Commons, sensing this shift in the public mood, took the opportunity and rejected Wilberforce's motion for further consideration of the abolition of the trade. The House of Lords' attitude was summed up by the member who declared flatly, "All Abolitionists are Jacobins."

The abolitionists' success was quickly reversed; lampooned in popular cartoons and ridiculed by critics, Wilberforce could have no hope of success.

One can only imagine the grief and frustration he must have felt. Perhaps he went home late one night and sat at his old oak desk, staring into the flame of a single candle. "Should I give up?" he might have thought. He sighed, flipping through his Bible. A thin letter fell from between the pages.

Wilberforce stared at the shaky handwriting. Its writer was dead; in fact, this letter was probably the last he had ever written. Wilberforce had read and reread it dozens of times, but never had he needed its message so deeply: "My dear sir," it began,

Unless the Divine power has raised you up to be as Athanasius contra mundum, I see not how you can go through your glorious enterprise, in opposing that execrable villainy, which is the scandal of religion, of England, and of human nature. Unless God has raised you up for this very thing, you will be worn out by the opposition of men and devils, but if God be for you who can be against you? Are all of them together stronger than God? Oh, be not weary of well-doing. Go on in the name of God, and in the power of his might, till even American slavery, the vilest that ever saw the sun, shall vanish away before it. That He that has guided you from your youth up may continue to strengthen in this and all things, is the prayer of,

Your affectionate servant,
John Wesley

"Be not weary in well-doing." Wilberforce's mind clicked; he took a deep breath, carefully refolded the letter, and blew out the candle. He needed to get to bed—he had a long fight ahead of him.

Wilberforce doggedly introduced motions each year for abolition; each year parliament threw them out. In late 1794 Wilberforce's advocacy for negotiating a peace in the war with France that had broken out the year before made him the subject of bitter public hostility. Even Pitt's friendship was temporarily shaken; the King disdained him, saying, "I always told Mr. Pitt they [the Clapham brothers] were hypocrites and not to be trusted." Others used this opportunity to heap derision on his chief cause, abolition, and circulated rumors that Wilberforce, unmarried at the time, was a wifebeater and that his wife was a former slave.

Another abrupt reversal came early in 1796, after the fall of Robespierre in France, with the swing of public sentiment toward peace. Fickle popular favor again turned toward Wilberforce, reinforced in a surprising majority vote in the House of Commons for his annual motion for abolition. With surprising swiftness, victory was suddenly within his reach.

Unfortunately the third reading of the bill took place on the night a long-awaited comic opera opened in London. A dozen supporters of abolition, supposing that the bill would surely be voted in this time, skipped parliament for the opera—and a grieving Wilberforce saw his bill defeated by just four votes.

So it went: 1797, 1798, 1799, 1800, 1801—the years passed with Wilberforce's motions, thwarted and sabotaged by political pressures, compromise, personal illness, and continuing war with France. By 1803, with the threat of imminent invasion by Napoleon's armies, the question of abolition was put aside for the more immediate concern of national security.

During those long years of struggle, however, Wilberforce and his friends never lost sight of their equally pressing objective—the reformation of English life.

John Wesley's indefatiguable preaching over fifty years had produced a great revival a half-century earlier, with its effect still being felt in many areas, particularly among the poor. But many individuals within the Church of England were Christian in name only, religion simply part of their cultural dress.

Wilberforce would not accept a perversion of Christianity which treated Christ as Savior but not Lord. Of church people he wrote, "If Christianity were disproved, their behavior would alter little as a result." Thus Sunday morning worship that did not manifest itself in daily holy living was hollow faith.

Given the prevailing attitudes of his day, Wilberforce knew he needed some dramatic ways to capture public attention and decided to ask King George III to reissue a "Proclamation for the Encouragement of Piety and Virtue and for the Preventing of Vice, Profaneness and Immorality." Though such proclamations were usually nothing but perfunctory political gestures, Wilberforce had discovered in his research that a similar statement issued by William and Mary had been used by local societies to successfully rally grass roots support. Wilberforce believed the same thing could be repeated in his day.

Backed by Pitt and others, Wilberforce's proposal went to the King, who issued his proclamation on June 1, 1787, citing his concern at the deluge of "every kind of vice which, to the scandal of our holy religion, and to the evil example of our loving subjects, have broken upon this nation."

Copies of the proclamation were distributed to magistrates in every county; Wilberforce mounted his horse and followed after them, calling on those in government and positions of leadership to set up societies to develop such a moral movement in Britain.

One prominent leader, Lord Fitzwilliam, laughed in Wilberforce's face—of course there was much debauchery and very little religion, he said, but after all, this was inevitable in a rich nation. "The only way to reform morals," he concluded, "is to ruin purses."

Even so, in many areas, the proclamation was received seriously. Magistrates held meetings to determine how to enforce its guidelines, and long-ignored laws were dusted off and enforced.

Significantly, in his quest for reform, Wilberforce did not ignore the brutal and inequitable penal system of his day, which prescribed capital punishment for such heinous offenses as stealing hares or cutting down trees—applied toward men, women, and children alike. He urged reforms in the "barbarous custom of hanging" though Wilberforce well knew that "regulating the outward conduct did not change the hearts of men." Reforming the general "spirit of licentiousness" by turning men and women to Christ could provide the only cure to crime.

Wilberforce and his colleagues were sensitive to their critics' charge that the proclamation would be applied vigorously against the poor without affecting the rich. "To expect to reform the poor while the opulent are corrupt," wrote Hannah More, the Christian playwright, "is to throw odours on the stream, while the springs are poisoned." So Wilberforce and his companions focused much of their efforts on their own peers in the upper classes. It was to good effect, as increasing numbers began to crowd long-empty churches.

The aristocracy was also infiltrated by young servants and governesses who were converted in the campaign. One such governess took a special interest in young Anthony Cooper, who would later become the Earl of Shaftesbury, the crusading Christian politician who courageously pioneered the most sweeping social reforms of the nineteenth century.

The young Princess Victoria, later to lead her nation as one of history's best-known monarchs, was also affected, having an Evangelical clergyman as her tutor. Later Victoria's ladies-in-waiting would gather for prayer each morning before breakfast, lifting up the young queen in her leadership of what by mid-century would once again become a God-fearing nation.

In the campaign against the slave trade, Wilberforce had seen the enormous impact that small pamphlets had in shaping public opinion. So he set out to collect on paper his deepening convictions about holy living. Taking advantage of a six-week recess late in 1796, he finished work on a book he had been formulating for years. The title told the story: *A Practical View of the Prevailing Religious System of Professed Christians in the Higher and Middle Classes in this Country Contrasted with Real Christianity.*

He completed it in early 1797; his publisher, skeptical about the sales potential of such a narrow religious book on the market of the day, greeted him with less-than-encouraging words: "You mean to put your name on the work?" Assured that Wilberforce did, the printer agreed on a cautious first run of 500 copies.

In a few days it was sold out. Reprinted again and again, by 1826 fifteen editions had been published in England and twenty-five in America, with foreign editions in French, Italian, Spanish, Dutch, and German. Republished in 1982, it remains a classic today.*

Wilberforce's friends were well-pleased. John Newton wrote, "What a phenomenon has Mr. Wilberforce sent abroad. *Such* a book by *such* a man and at *such* a time! A book which must and will be read by persons in the higher circles, who are quite inaccessible to us little folk, who will neither hear what we can say, nor read what we may write."

In *A Practical View*, Wilberforce presented a clear biblical message of salvation and a call to holy living, as opposed to the insipid "religion" so commonly practiced.

Wilberforce minced no words: to enter the Kingdom of God one must be born again. He wanted to impress his readers that "all men must be regenerated by the grace of God before they are fit to be inhabitants of heaven, before they are possessed of that holiness without which no man shall see the Lord." The true Christian is distinguished not by his church attendance but by his likeness to the holy, righteous Christ.

One prominent reader who skeptically picked up *A Practical*

---

*Real Christianity, Multnomah Press, 1982. Edited by Dr. James Houston, foreword by Senator Mark Hatfield.

View and ended up being converted by it said simply, "It led me to the scriptures." Countless thousands on two continents were similarly affected.

This book, written by a layman for laymen, revealed incredible theological insight and biblical understanding—evidence that Wilberforce had taken to heart the command to study, know, and trust the infallible word of God.

His growing spiritual maturity served him well in handling political pressures of his day. During the winter of 1797, when he differed with Pitt regarding the war with France, he wrote in his journal, "What conflicting passions yesterday in the House of Commons—mortification, anger, resentment—for such conduct in Pitt, though I ought to expect it from him and can well bear with his faults towards God—all these feelings working with anger at myself, from the consciousness that I was not what a Christian should be. . . . Yet even still I find my heart disposed to harbour angry thoughts. I have found the golden rule useful in quieting my mind putting myself in Pitt's place."

Wilberforce put into practice what he preached to others. Until his marriage in 1797, he regularly gave away a quarter of his income or more to the poor, Christian schools, and those in special need. He paid the bills of those in prison under the harsh debt laws of the day, releasing them to live productive lives; he helped with the pension for life given to Charles Wesley's widow. In 1801, when the war with France and bad harvests created widespread hunger, Wilberforce gave away £3,000 *more* than his income.

Since the group at Clapham were mostly political conservatives, it may seem ironic to some that they were constantly engaged in schemes to aid the oppressed. They organized the Society for the Education of Africans, the Society for Bettering the Condition of the Poor, the Society for the Relief of Debtors (which over a five-year period obtained the release of 14,000 people from debtors' prisons), to mention a few.

Various Clapham members were involved in prison reforms, hospitals for the blind, help for war widows and distressed sailors.

Zachary Macaulay, at one time worth £100,000, gave away all he had and died penniless.

That these two efforts—reforms of manners and abolition of the slave trade—remained linked through the years demonstrates the extraordinary spiritual insight of the Clapham sect. They understood the crucial interdependence of true spirituality and social reform: To attack social injustice while the heart of a nation remains corrupt is futile; to seek to reform the heart of a nation while injustice is tolerated ignores the lordship of Christ.

The years of battle had welded Wilberforce and the Clapham brothers into a tight working unit; with five of them serving as members of parliament, they exerted an increasingly strong moral pressure on the political arena of the day. Derisively labeled "the saints," they bore the name gladly, considering their persecution a welcome reminder of their commitment not to political popularity, but to biblical justice and righteousness. James Boswell's bit of snide verse shows the bitter abuse heaped on Wilberforce by his enemies.

Go, W— with narrow skull,
Go home and preach away at Hull.
No longer in the Senate cackle
In strains that suit the tabernacle;
I hate your little wittling sneer,
Your pert and self-sufficient leer.
Mischief to trade sits on your lip,
Insects will gnaw the noblest ship.
Go, W—, begone, for shame,
Thou dwarf with big resounding name.

Wilberforce and his friends were undaunted as they prepared for the fight in parliament in 1804. The climate had changed. The scare tactics of Jacobin association would no longer stick; and public sentiment for abolition was growing.

Thus the House of Commons voted for Wilberforce's bill by a

decisive majority of 124 to 49—but victory was short-lived. The slave traders were better represented in the House of Lords, which adjourned the bill until the next session.

In 1805, the House of Commons reversed itself, voting against abolition, rejecting Wilberforce's bill by seven votes. A well-meaning clerk took him aside. "Mr. Wilberforce," he said kindly, "You ought not to expect to carry a measure of this kind—you and I have seen enough of life to know that people are not induced to act upon what affects their interests by any abstract arguments." Wilberforce stared steely-eyed at the clerk. "Mr. Hatsell," he replied, "I *do* expect to carry it, and what is more, I feel assured I shall carry it speedily."

Wilberforce went home in dismay, his heart torn by the notion of "abstract arguments" when thousands of men and brothers were suffering on the coasts of Africa. "I never felt so much on any parliamentary occasion," he wrote in his diary. "I could not sleep after first waking at night. The poor blacks rushed into my mind, and the guilt of our wicked land."

Wilberforce went to Pitt to press for the cause. Pitt seemed sluggish; Wilberforce pushed harder, reminding him of old promises. Pitt finally agreed to sign a formal document for the cause, then delayed it for months. It was finally issued in September 1805; four months later Pitt was dead.

Wilberforce felt his death keenly, longing that he might have seen the conversion of his dear friend. He said, "I have a thousand times ... wished and hoped that he and I might confer freely on the most important of all subjects. But now the scene is closed—forever."

William Grenville became prime minister. He and Foreign Secretary Fox were both strong abolitionists; with their power behind it, the passing of Wilberforce's bill appeared now only a matter of time.

After discussing the issue with Wilberforce, Grenville reversed the pattern of the prior twenty years and introduced the bill into the House of Lords first, rather than the House of Commons. After a bitter and emotional month-long fight, at 4 A.M. on the morning of February 4, 1807, the bill passed.

It then went to the House of Commons. On the night of its second reading, February 22, a soft snow fell outside the crowded chambers. Candles threw flickering shadows on the cream-colored walls; the long room was filled to capacity but unusually quiet. There was a sense that a moment in history had arrived. A force more powerful than kings and parliaments and slavers' profits had triumphed; passions had been spent, and the moment was near that would mark the end of an epic twenty-year struggle.

Wilberforce, who had eaten supper earlier with Lord Howich, who was to introduce the bill, took his usual place quietly. He had written in his diary that morning with guarded confidence, "God *can* turn the hearts of men," but now, looking over the crowded room, he felt too aware of the defeats of the past to be certain of success.

Lord Howich, though an experienced speaker, opened the debate with a nervous, disjointed speech that reflected the tension in the chambers. Yet it did not matter; the opponents of abolition found they could do little to stem the decision about to be made.

One by one, members jumped to their feet to decry the evils of the slave trade and to praise the men who had worked so hard to end it. Speakers hailed Wilberforce and praised the abolitionists; Wilberforce, overcome, simply sat stunned. Waves of applause washed over him, and then as the debate came to its climax Sir Samuel Romilly gave a passionate tribute to Wilberforce and his decades of labor, concluding, "when he should retire into the bosom of his happy and delighted family, when he should lay himself down on his bed, reflecting on the innumerable voices that would be raised in every quarter of the world to bless him; how much more pure and perfect felicity must he enjoy in the consciousness of having preserved so many millions of his fellow-creatures."

Stirred by Romilly's words, the entire House rose, the members cheering and applauding Wilberforce. Realizing that his long battle had come to an end, Wilberforce sat bent in his chair, his head in his hands, unable to even acknowledge the deafening cheers, tears streaming down his face.

The battle was won. As one by one the members cast their votes for abolition, the motion was carried by the overwhelming majority of 283 to 16.

Late that night, as Wilberforce and his friends burst out of the stuffy chambers and onto the snow-covered street, they frolicked about like schoolboys, clapping one another on the back, their joy spilling over. Much later, at Wilberforce's house, they crowded into the library, remembering the weary years of battle, rejoicing for their brothers on the African coast. Wilberforce, the most joyous of all, turned to the lined face of his old friend Henry Thornton. They had worked through years of illness, defeat, and ridicule for this moment. "Well, Henry," Wilberforce said with joy in his bright eyes, "What do we abolish next?"

In the years that followed that night of triumph in 1807, a great spiritual movement swept across England like a fresh, cleansing breeze.

With the outlawing of the slave trade came an eighteen-year battle for the total emancipation of the slaves. Wilberforce continued as a leader of the cause in parliament as well as working for reforms in the prisons, among the poor, and in the workplace. In poor health much of the time, he watched many of his friends die as the years rolled by; others were raised up in their places. For though in the beginning of his crusade in 1787 he was one of only three members of parliament known as a committed Christian, by the end of his life more than 100 of his colleagues in the House of Commons and 100 members in the House of Lords shared that commitment.

Thus he could retire in 1825 knowing that God had raised up others to continue the fight. His health grew steadily worse; finally in late July, 1833, Wilberforce lay helpless on his bed.

On the night of July 26, the Bill for the Abolition of Slavery passed its second reading in the House of Commons, sounding the final death blow for slavery. Told the glad news, the old man raised himself on one boney elbow, then sank back, a quick smile crossing his lined face. "Thank God," he said, "that I should have lived to witness a day in which England is willing to give twenty millions sterling for the abolition of slavery!"

By the following Sunday he was in a final coma; and early Monday morning, William Wilberforce went to be with the God he had served so faithfully.

In the summer of 1978, my wife Patty and I were in London, where I was delivering a lecture series at All Souls Church. When I noticed a free evening in my schedule, I asked my hosts to arrange a visit to Clapham, the place where Wilberforce and the "saints" spent so much of their lives, praying, planning, and preparing for their glorious crusade.

Though I was a relatively new Christian, Wilberforce had already become a model for my life. Having experienced the lure of politics, power, and position, I well understood the kind of inner struggles he must have endured. When he anguished over his decision to follow Christ, he wrestled with the most fearsome dragon: "Pride is my great stumbling block," he wrote in his diary.

I wrestled with the same dragon that unforgettable night in August of 1973 when a friend shared with me how Christ, the living God, had changed his life. All at once, my achievements, success, and power seemed meaningless. For the first time in my forty years I realized that deep down in me was the most awful sin; I longed to be forgiven and cleansed. But the dragon of pride fought fiercely before it was slain in a flood of tears.

Wilberforce's life was also a magnificent inspiration for me in the ministry I had begun to prisoners. For his uncompromised commitment to Christ drove him all those years, one man taking his stand with a band of brothers for God's righteousness against the entire British Empire.

So I was anxious to visit the hallowed ground where Wilberforce and his friends had lived and worked.

A friend drove us through busy streets, heading south from the center of London. Clapham, in Wilberforce's time a peaceful village a few miles from the city, was long ago swallowed in the urban sprawl. We passed row after row of narrow, drab houses, and eventually came to the top of a small hill. "There it is," our friend exclaimed, pointing down a shabby street. "That's where Henry Thornton's house used to be!"

"Used to be?" I replied in disbelief. "Surely the Clapham sect's homes have been preserved as historic sites!"

"No," my friend shook his head. "Leveled long ago. People don't even know the exact location."

I was stunned and disappointed. In the States, one finds markers at the site of obscure battlefields, monuments to long-forgotten pioneers, the footprints of screen stars preserved in cement.

We drove several blocks to the Clapham green and stopped at an old soot-stained Anglican church. Our host had phoned ahead so the church rector was waiting to greet us.

"Wilberforce once preached in this pulpit," he announced proudly as he led me up a rickety flight of wooden steps to an ornately carved oak pulpit. For an instant I felt a twinge of excitement to stand where this slight, little man with his thundering voice had stood.

Painted in the center of a small stained glass window behind the altar was what the rector described as a "quite good likeness" of Wilberforce; I squinted but could barely make it out. "Is that all there is?" I asked, my disappointment deepening. "Oh, no!" the rector replied, leading me to a side wall where a small brass plaque was mounted in honor of the Clapham "saints." A pile of booklets about Wilberforce and his companions was stacked on a nearby table under a sign "50p apiece." That was it.

I'll never forget the scene, nor my emotions, as we left that little parish church. The cool, misty air sent chills through me. "After all those men accomplished," I mumbled, "surely more could have been done to honor their memory."

As we walked past the rows of dreary houses lining Clapham green, my host cautioned, "Not a good area to walk at night." It didn't matter; I felt I had already been robbed, somehow cheated.

Suddenly I stopped and stared across the green. In my mind's eye I began to see row upon row of black men and women walking right across the soft grass. I could hear the clanging of their chains as they fell from their arms and legs.

Of course, of course, I thought. Clapham is just what Wilberforce and his brothers would want. No spires of granite or marble rising into the sky. No cold statues or lifeless buildings in their honor. Rather the monument to Wilberforce and his friends is to be found in the freedom enjoyed by hundreds of millions of black people, liberated from bondage by a band of men who gave their all in following Christ.

Look at Africa today. It was Wilberforce and his friends who financed the first missionaries. Now Christianity, once the religion of the people's oppressors, is exploding across the continent, growing faster than anywhere else in the world.

The legacy of Wilberforce goes beyond even abolition and Africa. Taking a longer view of history, we can now see that he was a man standing in the gap at a crucial point in the history of Christendom—and the world. For in the late eighteenth century the age of reason dawned on the Continent. Humanist "enlightenment" was fast seizing the minds of the intelligentsia.

That is what sparked the bloody French Revolution. The revolution to end the unholy rule of divinely ordained tyrant kings would finally usher in man's utopia to reign on earth.

The main line of defense against the surging tides of enlightenment humanism had to be drawn in Britain. Where else? In the colonies, where a new nation was just taking root, fewer than 5 percent attended church. Rough frontiersmen had little time for religious niceties—and enlightenment writers like Thomas Paine were profoundly influencing America's founding fathers.

But Britain was, spiritually speaking, sinking sand. The church was apostate, the whole nation wallowing in self-indulgent decadence. But it was there that Wilberforce and his companions took their stand clinging to biblical truth, resisting barbaric injustice and striving to change the heart of a nation.

The eminent historian Will Durant once wrote that the great turning point of history was when "Christ met Caesar in the arena—and Christ won." Well might he have added that fifteen centuries later, Christ met vice and vested interests in Britain—and Christ won.

For out of Wilberforce's effort came a great spiritual movement in England. Social reforms swept beyond abolition to clean up child labor laws, poorhouses, prisons, to institute education and health care for the poor. Church attendance swelled. Evangelicalism flourished, and later in the century missionary movements sent Christians fanning across the globe. Christianity took such firm root in America as to convert a near-lawless frontier into a city upon a hill. The rising tides of enlightenment humanism were stemmed.

Monument to Wilberforce? Yes, the monument is a living legacy, found not only in the lives of millions of free men and women, but in the spiritual heritage of Christians everywhere.

Wilberforce has left a special legacy for today's Christians, caught up as so many are in the illusion that military might and political institutions are all-powerful. In the conclusion to his masterful book, *A Practical View*, Wilberforce wrote,

"I must confess equally boldly that my own solid hopes for the well-being of my country depend, not so much on her navies and armies, nor on the wisdom of her rulers, nor on the spirit of her people, as on the persuasion that she still contains many who love and obey the Gospel of Christ. I believe that their prayers may yet prevail."

Thomas Aquinas

by R.C. Sproul

R ECENTLY I WAS ASKED to identify my favorite theologians of all
time. I quickly named them: Augustine, Aquinas, Luther,
Calvin, and Edwards. Then I was asked to rate them according to
their brilliance. Being asked a question such as that is like being
asked to compare Babe Ruth with Mickey Mantle, or Johnny
Unitas with Dan Marino.

How does one rank the greatest minds of Christendom? Scholars
tend to differ in style and scope. The magnitude of their brightness
is as the stars in the Big Dipper. Luther was not systematic, yet he
gave awesome flashes of insight, powerful vignettes of vision that
changed the course of church history. Calvin possessed a systematic mind with the comprehensive grasp of theology that was
unprecedented. Augustine was surely the greatest theologian of
the first millenium of church history. Though his inconsistencies
are well documented, he is distinguished by being one who didn't
have the shoulders of giants to stand on. Rather, his shoulders bore
the weight of later giants, and some dwarfs as well.

Though it is fashionable to contrast Aquinas and Augustine as following the disparate paths of Aristotle and Plato, it is vital to remember that Aquinas leaned heavily on Augustine. It is probable that Aquinas quoted Augustine more frequently than he quoted any other theologian. Which theologian did Calvin quote more often than Augustine? None. Luther was an Augustinian monk and Edwards is sometimes referred to as a neo-Augustinian.

The historic debt of all these men to Augustine is so evident that it guarantees a special place to the bishop of Hippo in the gallery of stellar theologians. But who, we ask, was the brightest? Whose mind was most acute, most keen, most penetrating? If the question is posed in this manner, then I am forced into a corner with a two-forked exit. I cannot choose between the two men whose intellects most intimidate me, Edwards and Aquinas. To choose between them is to choose between Plato and Aristotle, of whom it was said that in the realm of philosophy all subsequent work achieved by men like Descartes, Locke, Hume, Kant, Wittgenstein, and others, is but a succession of footnotes.

So who was the most brilliant ever? I don't know. I know the question cannot be raised without the name of Thomas Aquinas being brought to the fore. And I know that he deserves my salute.

Those individuals whom history honors tend to receive awards or titles never pursued or coveted. Such a man was Aquinas. Of the many titles lavished on him, the D.A. degree stands out in particular. We are familiar with degrees and titles of Doctor of Philosophy, Doctor of Laws, and Doctor of Literature. We have Ph.D.'s, D.D.'s, M.D.'s, and Th.D.'s. But Thomas Aquinas alone bears the title *Doctor Angelicus.*

That Thomas was to be the Doctor of the Angels was not readily apparent to his school chums. His physique was unlike that of the stereotype theologian. Scholars are supposed to fit the mold of the frail, diminutive recluse, with bodies underdeveloped because of a sedentary life. Not so Thomas Aquinas. He was a big man, portly, suntanned, with a large head. He towered over his companions, no less in his massive physical bulk than in his titanic intellect. His appearance was so ungainly as a youth that he was dubbed "The big dumb ox of Sicily."

The best estimates of historians set the date of Aquinas' birth early in the year 1225. He was born in a castle near Naples, of noble parentage. He was the seventh son of Count Landulf of Aquino and Theodora of Theate.

His early years show indications that the hand of Providence was on his life. His predilection for theology was marked in childhood. At the tender age of five, an age when the modern child would be glued to the television set watching "Sesame Street," Aquinas was placed as an oblate in the abbey of Monte Cassino. There he mused on the nascent questions of ontology that gripped his mind for his entire life.

Thomas' father had big plans for his precocious son. Deeply embroiled in the political machinations between the Emperor and the princes of the church, Count Landulf sought the title of abbot for his son. Thomas politely but steadfastly refused. He borrowed a page from the life of his Lord and said, "It is better to obey the Father of spirits, in order that we may live, than the parents of our flesh." Thomas was committed to the service of God through the pursuit of an intellectual life. He was driven by an almost monomaniacal passion to answer the question, "What is God?"

At age fourteen Aquinas left the Benedictine abbey at Monte Cassino and was sent to Naples to study at the Faculty of Arts. There he came under the influence of the Dominicans and entered their order in 1244. His parents were not pleased by this decision and were further agitated when the Dominican General sought to send him to the University of Paris. On the way, Thomas was kidnapped by his own brothers and forced to return home. He was held captive by his own family for a year, during which he refused to abandon his habit and diligently kept the observances of his order every day. His zeal was so contagious that his sister was converted and his mother so impressed that, like the biblical Rebekah, she assisted her son in escaping from a window.

Thomas made his way to Paris where he first came under the tutelage of Albert the Great. Albert (Albertus Magnus) was to Aquinas what Socrates was to Plato. Albert poured his own titanic knowledge into the head of his most able disciple and followed his career with fatherly love. At the death of Saint Thomas, Albert was deeply grieved. Thereafter when Thomas' name was mentioned in Albert's presence, Albert would exclaim, "He was the flower and the glory of the world."

After three years of study in Paris, Albert took Thomas with him to begin a house of studies in Cologne. In 1252 Thomas returned to Paris. In 1256 he received his licentiate to teach in the faculty of theology. In 1259 he went to Italy and taught theology at the *studium curiae*, attached to the papal court until 1268. In 1268 he returned to Paris to take up the mighty controversy of his day, the controversy with Arab philosophy. In 1274 Pope Gregory X summoned him to assist in the Council of Lyons. On the journey Thomas' mission was interrupted by the angels. They came to take their Doctor home. At age forty-nine the earthly ministry of the dumb ox of Aquino had ended.

The most familiar title given Thomas Aquinas is that of "Saint." Though Protestants are likely to use the word "saint" as a synonym for any believer, following the New Testament usage, there are times when the most zealous Protestant will make use of the term to refer to someone who has achieved an extra level of spiritual maturity. In Rome the title is conferred by the church to a highly select few who have achieved a godliness considered above and beyond the call of duty.

When we think of Aquinas, our first thoughts are usually of his extraordinary gifts of scholarship. His was indeed a prodigious intellect, but his greatness at this point should not overshadow the spiritual power of the man. We might conjecture that his canonization was prompted by his intellectual contributions alone, but the record belies such an idea. Thomas was as noteworthy as a spiritual leader as he was for his theological acumen.

Within fifty years of the death of Aquinas the church conducted careful investigations into his personal life and teachings. Strong opposition to Aquinas' teaching set in early, and insults were hurled against his memory. But on July 18, 1323, at Avignon, Pope

John XXII proclaimed Thomas a saint. The Pope said of Aquinas, "Thomas, alone, has illumined the Church more than all the other doctors."

The modern theologian-philosopher, Jacques Maritain, was jealous to restore a high regard for Aquinas in the twentieth-century church. In his book titled simply *St. Thomas Aquinas*, Maritain rehearses the traditions of Aquinas' spiritual power and provides several anecdotes of alleged miracles that surrounded the saint. It was said of Thomas that though he contended fiercely in theological debates, he was able to bear personal attacks with a tranquil humility. Maritain relates the following:

> One day a Friar in a jovial mood cries out: "Friar Thomas, come see the flying ox!" Friar Thomas goes over to the window. The other laughs. "It is better," the Saint says to him "to believe that an ox can fly than to think that a religious can lie."

Witnesses who were summoned to testify at the canonization process of Saint Thomas described him as "soft-spoken, affable, cheerful, and agreeable of countenance, good in soul, generous in his acts; very patient, very prudent; all radiant with charity and tender piety; marvelously compassionate towards the poor." If we examine these virtues carefully, we see in them a litany of what the New Testament calls the fruit of the Holy Spirit.

Saint Thomas was also a gifted preacher. He would sometimes become so moved during his own preaching that he was forced to pause while he wept. During a Lenten series that he preached in Naples, he had to stop in the middle of his sermon so that the congregation could have time to recover from their weeping.

It is the mystical life of Saint Thomas, however, that has sparked the interest of biographers. Immediately after Thomas' death, his disciple Reginald returned to Naples and declared:

> As long as he was living my Master prevented me from revealing the marvels that I witnessed. He owed his knowledge less to the effort of his mind than to the power of his prayer. Every time he

wanted to study, discuss, teach, write or dictate, he first had recourse to the privacy of prayer, weeping before God in order to discover in the truth the divine secrets . . . he would go to the altar and would stay there weeping many tears and uttering great sobs, then return to his room and continue his writings.

A similar testimony comes from Tocco. He said of Aquinas, "His gift of prayer exceeded every measure; he elevated himself to God as freely as though no burden of flesh held him down. Hardly a day passed that he was not rapt out of his senses."

Being daily "rapt out one's senses" is hardly the routine we expect from abstract scholars and philosophers, particularly from someone like Aquinas who was given to the pursuit of logic.

The habit of passionate prayer is crowned by the extraordinary claims of miraculous visitations granted to Saint Thomas. Such incidents raise the eyebrows of Reformed theologians and we mention these accounts with the due reservations of our trade. Maritain recites the following episode as part of the Catholic record of Thomas' sainthood.

Another time it was the saints who came to help him with his commentary on Isaias. An obscure passage stopped him; for a long time he fasted and prayed to obtain an understanding of it. And behold one night Reginald heard him speaking with someone in his room. When the sound of conversation had ceased, Friar Thomas called him, telling him to light the candle and take the manuscript *On Isaias.* Then he dictated for an hour, after which he sent Reginald back to bed. But Reginald fell upon his knees: "I will not rise from here until you have told me the name of him or of them with whom you have spoken for such a long time tonight." Finally Friar Thomas began to weep and, forbidding him in the name of God to reveal the thing during Thomas' life, confessed that the apostles Peter and Paul had come to instruct him.

Another event occurred in Paris when Thomas was lecturing on the Eucharist. As he went to the altar the brethren suddenly saw Christ standing before him and heard Him speak aloud: "You have written well of the Sacrament of My Body and you have well and truthfully resolved the question which was proposed to you, to the extent that it is possible to have an understanding of it on earth and to ascertain it humanly."

That sober philosophers like Jacques Maritain report such incidences as simple historical fact is itself testimony to the extraordinary impact Aquinas' spiritual power had on his contemporaries as well as his future disciples.

One anecdote about St. Thomas is virtually beyond dispute. Toward the end of his life he had a powerful mystical experience that dramatically affected his work. Again we turn to Maritain for his account of it:

Having returned to Italy after Easter of 1272, Friar Thomas took part in the General Chapter of the Order, at Florence, and then he went to Naples again to continue his teaching there. One day, December 6, 1273, while he was celebrating Mass in the chapel of Saint Nicholas, a great change came over him. From that moment he ceased writing and dictating. Was the *Summa* then, with its thirty-eight treatises, its three thousand articles and ten thousand objections, to remain unfinished? As Reginald was complaining about it, his master said to him, "I can do no more." But the other was insistent. "Reginald, I can do no more; such things have been revealed to me that all that I have written seems to me as so much straw. Now, I await the end of my life after that of my works."

After this experience Thomas Aquinas wrote no more. On his final journey he asked to be taken to the monastery of Santa Maria. As he was dying he asked for Viaticum. When he saw the consecrated Host, he threw himself on the floor and cried out:

I receive Thee, Price of my redemption . . . Viaticum of my pilgrimage, for love of Whom I have studied and watched, toiled, preached, and taught. Never have I said anything against Thee; but if I have done so, it is through ignorance, and I do not persist in my opinions, and if I have done anything wrong, I leave all to the correction of the Roman Church. It is in this obedience to Her that I depart from this life.

There is a strange progression in the achievement of titles of honor and status in the theological world. A freshman student begins his pursuit of knowledge simply with his given name. When he graduates from college, some may now call him "Mister." When he graduates from seminary and passes his trials for ordination, he is granted the title "Reverend" or "Father." If he continues his education and achieves a doctorate, he is called "Doctor." If he is fortunate enough to secure a teaching position on a faculty, he must wait to progress to a full professorship. Then he can preface his name with the coveted title of "Professor." The irony is this: if he makes it really big and achieves a widespread reputation for his learning, he will achieve the highest honor, that of being known simply by his name. We do not usually speak of Professor Barth or of Doctor Calvin or Professor Küng. The leaders in the field of theology are known by their names. We speak of Barth, Bultmann, Brunner, Küng, Calvin, Luther, Edwards, and Rahner. A man doesn't seem to make it until his title returns to where he started, with his own name.

There is a special sense in which this strange progression reaches its acme with the titular honor paid to Aquinas. He is known not only by his famous last name, but in the world of theology and philosophy is recognized by his first name. No one speaks of Aquinasism. We talk about Calvinism, Lutheranism, Augustinianism, but with Aquinas it is Thomism. One need merely mention the name "Thomas" and every scholar of theology knows of whom we speak.

Think of all the Thomases there have been in the world. Think even of the Thomases who have been famous in Christendom.

There is "Doubting Thomas," Thomas a Kempis, Sir Thomas More, and a host of others. But only one theological giant is recognized instantly by the simple mention of the name "Thomas."

In 1879 a papal encyclical was issued in Rome by Leo XIII that praised the contribution of Thomas Aquinas. Leo declared:

> Now far above all other Scholastic Doctors towers Thomas Aquinas, their master and prince. Cajetan says truly of him: "So great was his veneration for the ancient and sacred Doctors that he may be said to have gained a perfect understanding of them all." Thomas gathered together their doctrines like the scattered limbs of a body, and moulded them into a whole. He arranged them in so wonderful an order, and increased them with such great additions, that rightly and deservedly he is reckoned a singular safeguard and glory of the Catholic Church. His intellect was docile and subtle; his memory was ready and tenacious; his life was most holy; and he loved the truth alone. Greatly enriched as he was with the science of God and the science of man, he is likened to the sun; for he warmed the whole earth with the fire of his holiness, and filled the whole earth with the splendor of his teaching. There is no part of philosophy which he did not handle with acuteness and solidity.

In the Code of Canon Law promulgated by Benedict XV, Catholic school teachers were ordered to "treat in every particular the studies of rational philosophy and theology, and the formation of students in these sciences, according to the method, the doctrine, and the principles of the Angelic Doctor, and to adhere religiously to them." Here Thomism is elevated to a supreme theological role in the church. Thomas moves beyond the scope of being *Doctor Angelicus* to the realm of being the Doctor of the Church *par excellence*, the Common Doctor of the faithful.

What then, is Thomism, the philosophy attached to the name of Aquinas? Is Thomism a philosophy or a theology? Was Thomas himself primarily an apologist or a theologian? Was he a biblical thinker or a speculative scholar who merely warmed over Aristotle and baptized his pagan philosophy? These are some of the questions that are evoked by the sound of Thomas' name.

The twentieth century has ushered in a revival of interest in Saint Thomas among Roman Catholic scholars. At the same time there has been a deepening cleavage between Roman Catholic Thomists and Evangelical Protestants. As Vatican Council I in 1870 looked to Protestantism as the fountain from which all modern heresies and distortions of truth flow, so modern Evangelicals have looked to the work of Thomas as being the poison that embittered the springs of truth.

The Protestant apologist, Norman Geisler (who at crucial points is pro-Thomas) is fond of quipping that "the new theme song of Evangelicalism is 'Should Old Aquinas Be Forgot, and Never Brought to Mind.'" On the other hand the late Francis Schaeffer was sharply critical of Saint Thomas, seeing in his work the foundations of secular humanism. He sees in Thomas' development of natural theology the magna charta of philosophy. With Thomas, philosophy was liberated from the controls of theology and became autonomous. Once philosophy became autonomous, separated and freed from revelation, it was free to take wings and fly off wherever it wished. Since Aquinas let the bird out of the trap, it has flown in the face of the faith. No longer is philosophy regarded as the handmaiden of Queen Theology but as her rival and possibly her destroyer.

Such an evaluation of Aquinas meets with resistance in some quarters of Protestantism. But the debate goes on. I, for one, am persuaded that the Protestant Church owes a profound debt to Saint Thomas and the benefit of a second glance at his contributions. I remind my Evangelical friends that when Saint Thomas defended the place of natural theology, he appealed primarily to the Apostle Paul and to Romans 1 for its classical foundation.

There is a sense in which every Christian owes a profound debt to Saint Thomas. To understand his contribution we must know something of the historical context in which he wrote. To gain a fair reading of any thinker, past or present, we must ask such questions as "What problems was he trying to solve? Why? What were the vibrant issues at stake in his day? What were the dominant controversies?" We know, for example, that throughout church history the development of theology has been prodded in large part by the threat of serious heresies. It was the heretic Marcion who made it necessary for the church to define the canon of sacred scripture. It was the heresy of Arius that provoked the council of Nicaea. It was the distortions of Nestorius and Eutyches that made the Council of Chalcedon necessary. The heat of controversy has been the crucible by which the truth of theology has been made more sharp, more lucid.

The threat to the church that awakened Saint Thomas from his own dogmatic slumber was one of the most serious challenges that Christendom has ever had to endure. Our present condition in the western world makes it a bit difficult to imagine the enormity of the threat. It was the rise and sweeping expansion of Islam that threatened Christianity in the thirteenth century. Our awareness of the threat tends to be limited to the more colorful and adventuresome element of it chronicled in the Crusades. Knights with crosses emblazoned on their chests riding out to free the Holy Land from infidels has a certain romance to it.

Saint Thomas also sought to rescue the Holy Land. Its walls were made of philosophical mortar. His lance was his pen and his coat of armor a monk's garb. For Thomas the war was a war of ideas, a battle of concepts.

Islamic philosophy had achieved a remarkable synthesis between Islamic religion and the philosophy of Aristotle. The powerful categories of Aristotelian thought became weapons in the arsenal of the two great Arab philosophers, Averroes and Avicenna.

The Islamic philosophers produced a system of thought called "integral Aristotelianism." One of the key points that flowed out of this was the concept of "double truths." The double truth theory allowed that certain ideas could, at the same time, be true in philosophy and false in theology. It was a remarkable achievement: the Arab philosophers were able to accomplish what no schoolboy could ever do despite the universal desire of schoolboys to do it—to have their cake and eat it too.

The problem with having one's cake and eating it too is obvious. If I save my cake, I cannot enjoy the taste of it while I am saving it. But if I eat it, then it is gone. I cannot save what is already gone. Seems simple enough. Philosophers, however, like lawyers, often have astonishing powers of making simple matters extremely complex, to the point that they think they can actually transcend the cake eating-saving dilemma. What's worse is they often have the rhetorical power to convince other people of their magic.

To translate the double truth notion into modern categories would look something like this: a Christian might try to believe on Sunday that he is a creature created in the image of God by the sovereign purposive act of a Divine Being. The rest of the week he believes that he is a cosmic accident, a grown-up germ that emerged fortuitously from the slime. On Wednesdays, however, he adopts a different standpoint. Wednesday is "Double-Truth Day." At prayer meeting on Wednesday, the Christian attempts to believe both viewpoints at the same time. One day a week he devotes himself to intellectual schizophrenia. He tries to believe and to live a contradiction. If he enjoys the game he might shoot for a long weekend of it until he gains the ultimate bliss and security of permanent residence in a lunatic asylum.

Aquinas was concerned not only to protect the Christian church from the attacks of Islam, but to protect mankind from intellectual suicide. He insisted that all truth is coherent. Reality is not ultimately chaotic. What is true in philosophy must also be true in theology. What is true in science must also be true in religion. Truth may be analyzed from different perspectives. Various disciplines may have specialized fields of inquiry, but Aquinas insisted that *all truth meets at the top.*

This cardinal principle of Aquinas presupposes some rather basic, though vitally important, axioms. It is based upon the prior conclusion that there is a God and that he is the creator of this world. The world is a universe. That is, the world is marked by diversity which finds its ultimate unity in God's sovereign creation and rule. The word "universe" as well as the term "university" comes from this mongrelized union of the two terms "unity" and "diversity."

The double truth theory destroys in principle the fundamental notion of a universe. The universe becomes a multiverse with no ultimate harmony or cohesion. Chaos is ultimate. Truth, as an objective commodity, becomes impossible. Here contradiction may be freely embraced at any time, and every day becomes Double-Truth Day.

One of Francis Schaeffer's most serious charges against Saint Thomas is the allegation that Thomas *separated* philosophy and theology. The charge is heard from other quarters as well, that Thomas separated *nature* and *grace*. Schaeffer's lament is that, since the work of Aquinas, philosophy has been liberated from her role as handmaiden to the Queen of the Sciences (Theology) and has now become theology's chief antagonist.

It is the prerogative of the theologian to make fine distinctions. One of the most important distinctions a theologian can ever make is the distinction between a distinction and a separation. (This is the kind of distinction that yields Excedrin headaches.) There is a crucial difference between distinguishing things and separating them. We distinguish between our bodies and our souls. If we separate them, we die. We distinguish between the two natures of Christ. If we separate them, we fall into gross heresy.

To *separate* philosophy and theology, nature and grace, was the last thing Thomas Aquinas ever sought to do. It was precisely the issue he was combatting. The double-truth theory separates nature and grace. Such a separation was the dragon Aquinas set out to slay. Aquinas was concerned to *distinguish* philosophy and theology, nature and grace, not to *separate* them. He came to bury Averroes, not to praise him.

Aquinas maintained consistently that ultimately there is no conflict between nature and grace. His posture was that grace does not destroy nature but fulfills it. What God reveals in the Bible does not cancel out what he reveals in nature. To be sure, it adds to the knowledge we can glean from a study of this world, but it does not contradict it.

Thomas taught that there are certain truths that can be discovered in nature that are not found in the Bible. To use a modern example, we cannot discover a blueprint for the circulatory system of the bloodstream in the Bible. Second Chronicles tells us very little about microchip computers. On the other hand, science can never teach us of the Trinity or of God's plan of redemption. The work of the Holy Spirit in the regeneration of a human soul cannot be detected with a microscope or x-ray machine.

Saint Thomas was simply stating what should be obvious, that we learn some things from nature that we can't learn from the Bible and we learn some things from the Bible that we cannot learn from nature. The two sources of information can never be ultimately contradictory. If they seem to contradict each other, then a warning buzzer should sound in our heads to alert us that we have made an error somewhere. Either we have misinterpreted nature, or misinterpreted the Bible, or perhaps we have misinterpreted both.

So far, so good. What has really raised the hackles of many modern Evangelicals is what Thomas said next. Thomas insisted that in addition to the specific information one can learn from nature and the information found only in the Bible, there is a field of knowledge that overlaps. There are truths that Saint Thomas called "mixed articles." The mixed articles refer to truths that can be learned either by nature or by grace.

The most controversial of the mixed articles is the issue of the existence of God. Clearly the Bible teaches that there is a God. Aquinas argues, however, that nature also teaches there is a God. There can be, therefore, a kind of *natural theology*. Natural theology means that nature yields a knowledge of God.

The question of natural theology and of proofs of God's existence drawn from nature has been a raging controversy in the twentieth century. We recall, for example, Karl Barth's rigorous rejection of natural theology in his debate with Emil Brunner. Theology in general and evangelical theology in particular has reacted severely to natural theology, seeing in it an intrusion of Greek philosophy into the household of faith. The dominant approach in our day is that of some variety of *fideism*. Fideism, which means literally "faithism," maintains that God can be known only by faith. God's existence cannot be established by philosophy. Nature yields no theology. The heavens may declare the glory of God, but such glory is never perceived except through the eyeglasses of faith.

Thomas appealed to the Bible for his defense of natural theology. He carefully reminded the Christians of his day that the Bible not only teaches us that there is a God, but that same Bible also teaches us that it is not the only source of that information. The Bible clearly and unambiguously teaches that men in fact not only can know, but *do know*, that God exists from his self-revelation in nature. Thomas simply reminded the church what the Apostle Paul labored to teach in the first chapter of the Epistle to the Romans.

When the modern Evangelical rejects natural theology in toto and adopts fideism as his standpoint, he becomes guilty of the very thing for which Aquinas is accused; he becomes guilty of separating nature and grace.

What is at stake here? Aquinas understood that fallen men and women will repeatedly seek to use the tools of philosophy and science against the truth of the Bible. However, he refused to surrender nature to the pagan. He refused to negotiate philosophy and science. Fideism is a policy of retreat. It hides behind a fortress of faith while surrendering reason to the pagan. It separates nature and grace in the worst possible way. The church becomes a cultural dropout; it seeks the sanctuary of the Christian ghetto. It seeks to reserve a safe place for the practice of worship, prayer, Bible study, and the like. In the meantime, art, music, literature, science, the university, and philosophy are surrendered to the pagan. If a Christian happens to be laboring in those endeavors, he is politely asked to live by a double-truth standard. Like the scientist who can't decide whether light is a wave or a particle, he is asked to believe that it is a "wavicle" or to believe that on Monday,

Wednesday, and Friday light is a wave; on Tuesday, Thursday, and Saturday it is a particle. (Of course on Sunday it rests.)

We are acutely aware that the church in our day has staggered under the assault of philosophers and scientists. There are few philosophers who see their task as being servants to the truth of God. There are few scientists today who see their task as "thinking God's thoughts after Him." Secular universities are not known for their gentle nurturing of Christian faith. The popular music charts do little to promote the kingdom of God. Modern art and literature are not communicating the beauty of holiness. No wonder that the church seeks a safe place of solace far removed from the battle-ground of culture.

We need an Aquinas. We need a titanic thinker who will not abandon truth for safety. We need men and women who are willing to compete with secularists in defense of Christ and of his truth. In this regard, the dumb ox of Aquino was heroic.

FIVE

Otto C. Keller

by W. Phillip Keller

D AD WAS ALWAYS, EVER, the Master's man. He saw himself clearly as the servant of the Most High. His intense loyalty to the living Lord Jesus Christ shaped his character. It directed his career. He was a man totally available to the purposes of God.

His unashamed love for Christ was the supreme secret of the remarkable impact of his rather brief life poured out for Africa. Though only an ordinary layman, he was incandescent, alight, bright, illuminating the pervading darkness of Africa early in this century.

He knew he was called to serve the sick and the suffering. He was a man sent to bind up the broken; to lift the downtrodden; to set free those enslaved by superstition, dark traditions, and grinding poverty.

No matter the cost of personal hardship, Dad never drew back from the call of duty. He was a man ready to comply at once with the Master's wishes. Because of such solid devotion to Christ, he was a formidable force in the rough and tumble frontier life of his times.

Not only was he a man dearly loved by God, but also a wonderful, warm human being beloved by his own family and claimed as a friend by untold thousands of Africans. Far and wide across the green hills and tawny plains of Kenya he was loved and esteemed as "The Beloved Bwana."

So engrossed was he in laying down his life for those to whom God called him, he seldom considered his own well-being. In twenty-eight years of tough service in the tropics, he took only two brief breaks. Little wonder most of the western world knew little of him.

He was a vital kernel of seed-grain planted by God in the stern soil of Africa that yielded a bountiful crop of remarkable results. He knew this. Nor did he ever seek for the applause and plaudits of his contemporaries in the civilized world. It was enough for him that he be a faithful servant for his beloved Master.

Just the smile of Christ's approval was all he desired.

Fame, recognition, human credentials were of little consequence. He had work to do for God and he would do it well. He had a life to be expended for others and he would live it gladly.

This brief biographical sketch is an honest attempt to portray the main features of this rather amazing person who was my earthly father. More than forty years have flowed down the stream of time since he passed on into the realm of rest in God. So it is possible to write with fairness, objectivity, and a certain degree of high regard that has not diminished across the intervening spans of time.

Dad was the eldest son in a family of nine children. Reared in the plain, austere environment of a rural pastor's home, he early learned what it meant to do without all the niceties of life.

Still there was instilled in him a quiet loyalty to God, a pressing need to serve others for fulfillment, a deep love for the land, and an intense determination to do one's very best for the Master, no matter how mundane the task.

He was the first to leave home to find work in the rough and tumble of middle America. Open honesty, total reliability, energetic work, and keen foresight soon assured him of success in the construction industry.

By his early twenties he was what they call a "self-made man," living in upper Michigan. But in his own soul Dad was wise enough to know that every ability he possessed to prosper was a direct gift from his Father in heaven.

He was not blinded by self-conceit or personal pride. His character was not tarnished with the self-importance of a self-centered individual. He recognized he was endowed with special aptitudes for service. These he was eager to put at the Master's disposal.

The direction in which he was to move came into clear, sharp focus through the death of his closest and dearest friend. This young man and his beautiful bride had gone out to German East Africa (now Tanzania) as simple lay missionaries. In calm faith they, along with another single man, had felt called to serve in this remote area.

The German authorities assigned them a tribe to work among in a drought-ridden region. For lack of surface water, the two young men dug a deep well. In ecstatic delight they struck a seep of water. But there was death in the seemingly precious liquid.

Within days the two young men were dead.

Only by a miracle of divine intervention, and her own sturdy constitution, did the young bride survive.

Strong, not only in her physical body, but also bouyantly brave in her confidence in Christ, she stayed on for another five years of full-hearted service in the bush.

When the shattering news finally drifted out of the African bush and back to Michigan, it simply galvanized the successful young businessman into action. If his friend could lay down his life for Africa, so would he. In a matter of weeks he disposed of his business, took his assets, and set sail. It was 1914.

To recount these events on paper, some seventy years later, is rather simple. But for Dad to take such bold steps without the support of any human agency or organization was an act of enormous courage.

Turning away from his family, his associates, his thriving business, his promising future, he set his will like a shaft of steel to do whatever God called him to do in serving Africa amid its agony.

It was a demonstration of formidable faith in his heavenly Father, a quiet confidence in Christ, a sure trust that God's guiding Spirit would lead him.

On board ship, the young, eager bachelor was befriended by a Quaker doctor and his wife en route to open a hospital for the Friend's Society near the shining waters of Lake Victoria. It was the beginning of a profound companionship that would endure a lifetime.

As their slow ship moved along the hot, sultry coast of the great brooding continent, World War I erupted in Europe. As a consequence, fierce fighting also broke out in the African bush between the German and British colonial forces. By the time the steamer docked in Mombasa all passengers for East Africa were put ashore. None would be disembarking at Dar es Salaam in German territory.

Dad, in his usual decisive manner, immediately offered his services to the British authorities in Kenya. They promptly appointed him to serve in famine relief. For months the country had endured a formidable drought, similar to that now scourging the continent. Overnight he was plunged into the awesome anguish of forlorn people perishing all around him. He was to be cast into the crucible of a furnace of human suffering that would shape the contours of his entire life.

He was sent some 600 miles inland to a station near the shores of Lake Victoria. Happily this location was close to where the doctor and his wife would work. And there Dad literally buried himself amid the starving and dying natives that poured into the post from their devastated reserves.

In their agony he learned to love the tribe's people with a deep compassion and touching tenderness seldom matched among Europeans. He knew what it was to weep as they wept; to groan with hopeless agony as mothers groan who have no milk for their whimpering babes; to look with sun-seared eyes for some sign of rain that never came; to feel the utter hopelessness of a land and people perishing for lack of food and lack of loving care.

Standing there amid the surging masses of men and women with hands outstretched for a handful of cornmeal or a spoonful of beans, Dad became in truth a father to the fatherless, a friend to the forlorn, a tower of hope to those without hope.

Amid the chaos and despair he seldom heard a single word of English spoken. The sounds that came to him were a cacophony of various dialects. Yet in ways shaped by the trauma of his times his ears were attuned to the strange languages that engulfed him from dawn to dark. In a remarkably short span of time he became uniquely gifted in the local languages.

To the unbounded delight of the Africans he could converse with them fluently. He knew their colloquialisms. He understood the subtleties of their parable forms. He could even share the gentle mirth of their humor; his wit, like theirs, was a balm of refreshment to weary spirits.

But even more amazing were the bridges of love and bonds of affection built between this newcomer and his newfound friends. It was along these paths he brought them the love of God.

In the pain and pathos of the famine relief, God had given my father an open entrance into thousands of African hearts. There he shared unashamedly in the suffering of Christ. And so in the outpouring of his own life there was shed abroad the compassionate care of the living Lord. In one hand he brought maize meal, salt, beans and cups of cold water; in the other he bore the great good news of Christ's amazing love for these perishing people.

The famine dragged on month after month. The skies blazed with burning heat. The grass was gone. Trees withered and died. Streams and springs became desolate trenches filled with dust.

Then one day electrifying news ran along the human grapevine of the African community. Word had come that a remarkable, young, single, white woman had trekked across 256 miles of the Tanzania bush country. She was headed for the lake and hoped to return home to Canada by way of Kenya.

Dad wondered if it might possibly be the widowed young bride of his best friend. He went down to meet the next little lake steamer that came to shore. Sure enough on board he found the gallant girl, smitten by sunstroke, totally delirious, at the point of death.

He rushed her to the nearest mission hospital and there made arrangements for her long convalescence. She had been plucked from the edge of death as by a miracle of God's grace.

As time permitted Dad visited the young woman. Bit by bit her strength returned; so, too, did her vivacious charm, her joyous good humor, her shining spirit. She knew she had been spared to serve Africa.

Friendship flourished into warm affection. And so, by degrees, my father wooed and won her heart and love.

The engaged couple felt it was only fair that she should first return to her family for a brief visit before they were married. This called for great faith since the German U-boats, fierce marauders of the sea, had destroyed so many ships. Yet in spite of all the obstacles, my father's fiancée crossed the Indian and Pacific oceans to be reunited with her family again.

It was as though she had been resurrected from the dead. This quiet demonstration of God's care for her all through the war years was a means of moving the whole family to put their trust in Christ.

Soon she would return to East Africa where in the meantime Dad was making some long-range decisions. The famine years had ended. The rains had returned. There was grain in the bins and grass on the hills. Singing, laughter, and light-hearted banter filled the lives of those who had survived the scourge of the long drought.

For my father this respite from the famine relief set him free to move from station to station, serving as interim caretaker while the white workers went on leave. It gave him a profound insight into the methods used by various mission societies to establish a church in Africa.

He was convinced there were better ways to achieve great things for God than the stereotyped style of mission work common in those times. He was farsighted enough to see that a robust African church had to be built with people who were not only revitalized in spirit, but also sound in body, strong in mind, and socially stable.

Only thus could the indigenous church flourish.

He was wise enough to know that the whole fabric of native life needed to be rewoven with vision and faith in God.

What he needed was a piece of land where such a work could be started. In his search he found a block of 110 acres of rocky ground on a height of land overlooking the lake seven miles away. It was a property abandoned by a would-be missionary who had turned hippo hunter. Yet it was a strategic site of God's arrangement.

Dad purchased it for a nominal price. On the surface it appeared a waste of scrub grass, brush, and rocks, haunted by hyenas, jackals, and wild game. Only one crude mud and wattle structure stood on the site.

But he could see beyond all of this. He could see down the long avenues of the years ahead when there would stand in this spot one of the most dynamic spiritual endeavors in all of East Africa. Here the life and power of the living Christ would outshine all the darkness around it.

Then one day, after a year of waiting, Dad took the rickety train down to the coast to welcome back his radiant fiancée. Without pomp or ceremony, the keen young pioneers were married in a magistrate's office. The two returned to set up their home in the mud house on the barren hill.

A year later I was born, delivered in the stygian darkness of the African night by the beloved Quaker doctor who had become Dad's dearest friend. A simple coal oil lantern supplied light. And warm water for washing was heated over an open wood fire in an empty kerosene tin. This was to begin life at rock bottom level.

Yet for my parents it was all an enormous and thrilling adventure in company with Christ. Their quiet, implicit confidence in his care for them was a legacy given to me as a small child that remains a timeless treasure. They simply trusted God their Father for every aspect of life. It was he who had brought them to this spot. He would keep them here. He would lead them on from here. All was well!

There never was a sense of drudgery or boredom or ennui about my parents. They were a couple intensely in love with one another, in love with the land of their adoption, in love with the Africans, in love with the Lord.

Dad was full of humor. It was one of his great saving graces, bestowed upon him by God to face the formidable challenges of his times. He was a master storyteller. His ability to recount some of the outrageous events of his colorful career would convulse his friends in mirth.

A typical tale involved the time when, as a bachelor, he went to the little kitchen unexpectedly to see what his young Marigoli cook was preparing for supper. To his utter astonishment and chagrin he found the lad straining the hot soup through one of his own socks.

When he remonstrated with the would-be chef that this simply was not done, the dear fellow, all embarrassed, blurted out: "Oh, but Bwana, please do not get angry, I did not use your clean socks!"

The constant impression that came to me as a small lad was that Dad, Mother, and God were all caught up in an exciting adventure together. Life was full of fresh advances. It abounded with new endeavors. New frontiers were being opened with faith and optimism.

These found form and substance in a dozen different ways against a background of primitive paganism steeped in animism and spirit worship. The blazing contrast between the crude and cruel culture of the natives around our home and the shining exhilaration of my parents was as clear-cut as night and day—death and life—despair and love.

Despite all the protestations of modern anthropologists, the fact remains that the Africans to whom Dad came as the Master's servant were sunk in debauchery and total degradation of the darkest hues. Witchcraft, superstition, and shrinking fear of evil spirits shackled the souls of the natives around our home. Most of the men and women were draped scantily in skins taken from their goats, sheep, or wild game. Their bodies were adorned with beads, massive coils of wire and fantastic arrays of feathers. To the uninitiated they appeared ferocious. But to Dad and Mother they were friends trapped in the tyranny of their own tribal traditions and grinding poverty.

Most of the men were notoriously indolent. Given to excessive debauchery they lolled in the shade of scrubby trees most of the day, then spent their nights in ribald revelry. They would stagger past our place shouting and chanting in the darkness, hoping to drive away the demons they dreaded.

Women were abused and maltreated as though of less value than even a dog or donkey. They not only bore the babies, most of whom perished in infancy, but also bore the entire work load of digging, planting, harvesting, gathering wood, and carrying water in clay pots on their heads.

It never ceased to astonish me how brutal was the behavior of the men in beating their wives and children. Throughout the nights the throb of the beer drums, the animal-like shouts of intoxicated men, all mingled with the screams of women and children beaten with clubs and whips.

The huts and villages built of mud and sticks, plastered with cow dung, were crude and filthy hovels in which human beings, goats, chickens, and a few scrub cattle lived together at a bestial level. With utter boldness and unflinching courage, Dad and Mother entered these places to bring help and healing. Their love and compassion was shed abroad so freely in their visits that many of the villagers were drawn from their despair to discover a new life in God.

The piece of land which Dad purchased held three remarkable assets which drew people to it from far and wide. First of all it had the only permanent water spring in that barren part of the hills. So women and children congregated there from miles around to fill their pots. These they bore away brimming full to huts scattered far and wide across the countryside. En route they passed our house.

Second, the property lay adjacent to the largest local native market. So tribe's people with every sort of produce gathered here to barter their corn and sweet potatoes for eggs, meat, or honey. Sitting on the ground, their goods spread around them, they would argue and haggle in the sun for a scrap of hide or handful of beads or a bleating goat. It was a noisy, colorful scene that drew hundreds of Africans to the environs of our home.

Third, this site to which Dad was sure he had been directed by his heavenly Father was like the hub of a wheel. For it was the center of conjunction at which the boundaries of four distinct tribal groups came together. To the west were the Luo people of Nilotic descent. To the north were the Marigoli of Bantu origin. To the east were the Kipsigis and Nandi of Hamitic stock. To the south was an enclave of Somalis with their Islamic traditions from the east coast.

All of these diverse people in their coming and going; in their intertribal trade; in their eternal search for wood, water, and food passed by our place. And what they saw and heard and touched there, astonished them. Before their own eyes they saw amazing changes taking place. Changes that became the main theme of the chatter in their village circles, changes that would touch and transform their own way of living, changes that would alter the appearance of the whole countryside.

From the outset Dad was regarded with a double sense of awe and affection. News of his long years of famine relief had reached these people along the grapevine of native gossip. They knew him as a friend of those in need. But beyond this his remarkable fluency in their own dialects, his sense of fun, his enormous energy, and his unbounded empathy for the Africans drew them to him.

One of his first achievements was to help protect them from predators. Leopards and hyenas were taking a heavy toll of sheep, goats, and calves. In the patchwork gardens, troops of baboons, monkeys, and warthogs devastated the meager crops. Dad was a superb marksman and formidable hunter in the finest frontier tradition. So the natives soon learned they could count on him to help save their stock and crops from total ruin whenever wildlife depredation was excessive.

As a small lad, I often heard the low growl of leopards on the prowl around our house. At dawn we often found the remains of a goat, a calf, or a wild buck lodged in the limbs of the great mussengeli tree in our front yard. The insane howl of hyenas and staccato yaps of jackals punctured the nights.

Very quickly Dad and Mother set up a small, sparkling medical dispensary back of the house. Word of this fanned out across the country. The region was notorious for its diseases. Malaria, intestinal dysentary, rickets, ugly ulcers, and other disorders were endemic. Most of the people were old by their forties, many dead by their fifties, because of malnutrition.

Dad was wise enough to know that the remedy for all of this was more, much more, than medicine and bandages and hospital beds. It would mean improved hygiene, better crops, proper soil management, upgrading of livestock, and the conservation of natural resources.

Poor soils make poor people the world over.

Nor can a virile, strong community of Christians be built upon a population with eternally empty stomachs and disease-ridden bodies. Dad was thirty years ahead of his times in seeing this.

Christ had come into the world to do the Father's work in ministering to the whole of man. So would he!

With almost terrifying single-mindedness of soul and spirit he and Mother flung themselves into the work of turning a rock-girt chunk of the African bush into a magnificent mission for the honor of God.

Using muscular teams of oxen hitched to plows and steel-wheeled wagons such as these people had never seen, he worked the wild land with care. Thousands of tons of stone and rock were removed from the soil to be used in erecting a sturdy stone house, graneries, workshops, and a magnificent building for worship and classes.

Dad taught the Africans how to cut stone, chisel rock, and lay up straight handsome walls resistant to termites. He instructed them in making brick from the rich clay anthills that dotted the country. The skills of building brick kilns, firing them, and using the end product were all skills shared with the Africans.

He set up workshops where apprentice lads could learn to be

first-class carpenters. They became skilled in sawing logs, shaping timber, handling tools, building beds, benches, tables, doors, and windows for new homes and burgeoning buildings of all sorts.

The stirring, exciting, captivating changes on the hill drew a constant stream of people to our place. It was not a show. It was not a pantomime. It was a profound metamorphosis of life in which they took a personal part.

The transformation of the land itself was even more arresting for the natives than had been the buildings. Dad worked with the inspired fervor of a Luther Burbank. He knew that this soil beneath his bush boots was capable of prodigous production if only the proper crops, grasses, and trees suited to the tropics could be found.

He was hard-headed enough and spiritually sensitive enough to realize that his Father above was as concerned about corn in the field as a crop of spiritual fruit in the souls of his starving people.

With enormous energy and unflinching foresight Dad sent all over the world for improved plant material. He imported the first hybrid corn seed from America. He brought in improved vegetable varieties from Britain. He sent for stocks of exotic fruit trees from South Africa. He introduced scores of different species of eucalyptus trees from Australia. He planted new and superior strains of grass and legume cover crops to heal the eroded barren land.

The natives were taught new ways to till and improve the soil. They were shown how to terrace and contour their land. Dad shared the new seeds and cuttings and seedlings from the abundance of his own prodigious efforts. He wanted the Africans to share in the beautiful bounty of what their own land could produce.

He was utterly opposed to the concept of making "rice Christians" as had been done in the Orient, or "Kaffir-corn Christians" as had been the case in Africa. He had such incredible respect for the inherent intelligence of the natives that he refused to make them eternal recipients of western charity. They needed, as we all do, a sense of self-esteem and personal achievement.

Dad was determined he would assist Africans to stand tall on their own territory. He would help them to help themselves.

In passing it should be stated that what Dad was doing in the fields and gardens and woodlots, Mother was doing in the homes of these astonished and awe-struck people. She had classes in child care, in simple hygiene, in improved nutrition, in sewing of fresh garments, in singing, reading, and writing.

It was as if a yeast of renewal and rejuvenation was at work in that desolate corner of the weary old world. She was a fearless frontier woman who with her hearty laughter and indomitable spirit brought light and life and love into the hearts of a hundred homes around us.

Dad had enormous respect for her. The two of them, like a tremendous team in harness together, were achieving extraordinary exploits in company with Christ.

In due course an improved road was built from the shores of the lake, inland to the cool highlands. An increasing influx of would-be settlers, gold miners, and traders hoping to make their fortunes in this frontier passed our home. Scores of strangers came through our place along this rocky African road.

They would stumble into the grounds astonished at the gorgeous beauty of the flowers and shrubs cascading over the gardens. They marveled at the splendid livestock grazing in the pastures. They were taken aback by the abundance of fruit and vegetables. They saw joyous Africans everywhere.

Not one stranger was ever turned away from our door. I recall again and again finding as many as a dozen guests seated at the great round table in our home. To all of them Dad and Mother gave and gave and gave of their strength, their love, and their compassion.

This in essence was the warp and woof of the fiber of their lives. They lived for others. They saw themselves as servants of the Most High. They were at Christ's command.

There was no pretext or pompous pride in Dad's makeup. He never behaved toward the Africans in a patronizing way. With their profound capacity to see clearly into and through human character, the natives recognized in this man qualities of loyalty, love, and esteem that they found in very few white people.

Dad never put himself on a pedestal. He did not pretend to be what he was not. He was simply "the Master's man." He never sought recognition or plaudits from his peers. He had an enormous job to do for God, and he got on with it. It was sufficient for him to please Christ and be a benefit to others around him.

This whole approach to life was the very heart of the way in which he spoke to others about God. He did not preach in that stilted and perfunctory manner so common to those of the cloth. He did not indulge in highbrow dissertations about abstract ideas. He was a lay person, chatting with lay people, about the character and conduct of his closest friend, the living Christ. It was this One whom he wished others to meet and know. It was this One whom he wanted them to trust and love. It was this One whom he desired above all else that they should learn to enjoy during their short years on earth.

Whenever he spoke to the Africans, he used parables just as Jesus did. He couched his remarks in vivid word pictures that were readily grasped and long remembered. He spoke much of water, grain, seed, soil, sheep, and cornmeal. These were the languages of the land but also the stepping stones that led the soul to lay hold of spiritual truth.

It was in the searching, seeking, thirsty souls of his hearers that such a sharing of God's amazing love took root. Africans by the hundreds came to hear the great good news of the compassion of Christ, of his forgiveness, of his freedom from their fears.

The church building which he first erected was no longer large enough to accommodate the crowds that came. A larger edifice had to be erected. Then in time people began to request that other churches and schools be started in their distant locations.

When I was a teenager it reminded me of a pebble dropped in a pond. The resulting ripples spread out wider and wider to move and touch the whole of society. The great good news was stirring spirits, changing lives, bringing hope and health and abundant goodwill wherever it went.

Africans were entering not only the family of God, but they were entering the twentieth century. They were keeping better livestock with surplus meat and milk to sell. They were planting groves of trees that sheltered the soil and supplied surplus wood for fuel and logs for lumber. They were building better homes, schools, shops, and storehouses of brick and stone. They had skilled services to offer as carpenters, bricklayers, stonemasons, and teamsters. They were growing superior crops of corn, fruit, vegetables, and grain to nourish their own flourishing families. This also encouraged a thriving trade with others.

On the sound basis of improved land management and enhanced human nutrition a whole new generation of keen and energetic young people began to emerge. They crowded into the classrooms. They built their own new schools, staffed with well-trained teachers. The same held true for the churches that sprang up swiftly, like mushrooms after the rains, one after another across the hills and plains.

It was all tremendously inspiring. I would come home on holidays from the wretched, boring boarding school I was obliged to attend, and find Dad ecstatic about the winds of change that were sweeping across the country under the impact of God's generous Spirit.

For a while there were sixteen churches, then fifty, then well over a hundred, and finally more than three hundred.

In his own sovereign generosity God saw fit to perform a mighty work of renewal among the Africans. In deep contrition and open confession they sought reconciliation with Christ and one another. Wrongs were put right and whole families flourished in their newfound freedom.

As the years went by Dad devoted more and more of his time and strength to instructing outstanding African youths to become the leaders of their own people. He was totally convinced that the African church was fully capable of being self-governing, self-supporting, self-perpetuating. And in fact subsequent events have proved him right. For in Kenya today there is perhaps the highest percentage of eager, enthusiastic Christians in the population to be found anywhere in the world.

He was not reluctant to relinquish leadership in the church to capable Africans. He was eager to see keen native leaders emerge. He was sure that God's grace, wisdom, courage, and guidance could be bestowed on a black man just as surely as on his white brother. This concept few in the United States today will concede, despite all the hypocritical talk of equal rights and equal opportunity in our society.

The net result was that God honored Dad's devotion to his duty as few men have been honored. First of all I give it as my own personal witness that never did I ever see such steady transformation in any person's life as his. The grace of God, the touch of the Master's hand, the gentle influence of God's gracious Spirit were so apparent in his character and conduct that for me as a growing youth it was an ongoing miracle. He was my hero! No one ever moved me more to live only for God and the benediction of my generation.

His was a totally selfless life poured out for others. He gave and gave and gave that others might gain life. This in essence is the very life of God, the love of Christ, demonstrated in the brief, shining life of a common man.

When he died at the comparatively young age of fifty-four, it was the dear Quaker doctor who buried him in the warm soil of the land he loved so well. Dad left behind a legacy of over 500 African pastors and evangelists with uncounted thousands upon thousands of joyous Christians under their care. He had come to Kenya as a common layman in its hour of despair. He left with the honor and majesty of God's mighty presence sweeping across the country.

HE WAS THE MASTER'S MAN!

SIX

David Martyn Lloyd-Jones

by J.I. Packer

D AVID MARTYN LLOYD-JONES, the "Doctor" as he was called in public by all who knew him (even his wife!), resigned in 1968 after thirty years as pastor of London's Westminster Chapel. He died on St. David's Day, March 1, 1981. He was the greatest man I have ever known, and I am sure that there is more of him under my skin than there is of any other of my human teachers. I do not mean that I ever thought of myself as his pupil, nor did he ever see himself as my instructor; what I gained from him came by spiritual osmosis, if the work of the Holy Spirit can be so described. When we met and worked together, as we did fairly regularly for over twenty years, we were colleagues, senior and junior, linked in a brotherhood of endeavor that for the most part overrode a quarter of a century's difference in our ages.

It was a shared concern that first brought us together: I, who did not know him, went with a friend who did in order to ask if he as a Puritan-lover would host and chair a conference that we hoped to mount on Puritan theology. He did so, and the conference became an annual event. Other shared concerns—explaining evangelicalism to the British Council of Churches; the now-defunct *Evangelical Magazine;* Reformed fellowships and preaching meetings; the quest for revival—these kept us together from 1949 to 1970. For me it was an incalculably enriching relationship. To be wholly forthcoming, genial, warmhearted, confidential, sympathetic, and supportive to ministerial colleagues of all ages was part of the Doctor's greatness. It was, I think, a combined expression of his Presbyterian clericalism, based on the parity of all clergy, plus his feeling as a physician for the common dignity of all who have charge of others' welfare, plus the expansive informality of the Welsh family head. It was an attitude that left countless ministers feeling like a million dollars—significant in their calling, purposeful about it, and invigorated for it. The Doctor's magnetic blend of clarity, certainty, common sense, and confidence in God made him a marvelous encourager, as well as a great molder of minds. He was a pastor of pastors *par excellence.* He would have hated to be called a bishop, but no one ever fulfilled towards clergy a more truly episcopal ministry. I know that much of my vision today is what it is because he was what he was, and his influence has no doubt gone deeper than I can trace.

To be sure, we did not always see eye to eye. Over questions of churchly responsibility we were never on the same wavelength, and this led eventually to a parting of the ways. Ironically, what made our head-on collision possible was the conviction we had in common, which for many years had bound us together and distinguished us from many if not most of England's evangelicals. What these convictions added up to was a consuming concern for the church as a product and expression of the gospel. We both saw the centrality of the church in God's plan of grace. Both of us believed in the crucial importance of the local congregation as the place of God's presence, the agent of his purposes, and the instrument of his praise. We both sought the church's spiritual unity, internal and external—that is, oneness of evangelical faith and life, appearing in a unanimous Bible-based confession and a challenging Spirit-wrought sanctity. Both of us sought the church's purity—the elimination of false doctrine, unworthy worship, and lax living. We both backed interdenominational evangelical activities, not as an ideal form of Christian unity, but as a regrettable necessity due to the inaction of the churches themselves, which made it certain that if parachurch bodies did not do this or that job it would never get done at all. Had these convictions not been so central to both our identities, we should not have clashed as we did.

The possibility of an explosion was there from the start. I was English and Anglican and the Doctor a Welsh chapel-man to his fingertips. He had little respect for Englishness, or for Anglicanism as a heritage or Anglicans as a tribe. (He saw the English as pragmatists, lacking principle, and Anglicans as formalists, lacking theology. When he told me that I was not a true Anglican he meant it as a compliment.) His world was that of seventeenth-century Puritans, the eighteenth-century Evangelicals, and nineteenth-century Welsh Calvinists. It was a world of bare chapel walls and extended extempore prayer; of preachers as prophets and community leaders; of spiritual conversions, conflicts, griefs and joys touching the deep heart's core; of the quest for power in preaching as God's ordinary means of enlivening his people; and of separation to start new assemblies if truth was being throttled in the old ones. In all of this the Doctor was a precise counterpart of the Baptist, C.H. Spurgeon, who himself fulfilled an awesome ministry of Puritan evangelical type in London nearly a century earlier. The only difference was that Spurgeon learned his nonconformity not in Wales but in East Anglia. I never heard the Doctor described as Spurgeon *redivivus*, but the description would have fitted. Like Spurgeon, he thought Anglicanism discredited and hopeless. To look for genuine, widespread evangelical renewal in the Church of England seemed to him "midsummer madness," (his phrase), and he was sure that in doing this that I was wasting my time. "They won't accept you," he used to tell me, and it was plain that he hoped eventually to see me leave the Anglican fold.

Denominationalism finally became the break-point. Officially a minister of the Presbyterian Church of Wales, the Doctor had become a convinced Independent, viewing each congregation as a wholly self-determining unit under Christ, in the Spirit, and before God. In the 1960s he began to voice a vision of a new fellowship of evangelical clergy and congregations in England that would have no links with "doctrinally-mixed" denominations, that is, the Church of England, the English Methodist Church, and the English Baptist Union. To winkle evangelicals out of these bodies he invoked the principle of secondary separation, maintaining that evangelicals not only were free to leave such denominations but must do so, for they were guilty by association of all the errors of those from whom they did not cut themselves off ecclesiastically. Opposing and repudiating those errors, so he urged, does not clear one of guilt unless one actually withdraws. Because my public actions showed that I disagreed with all this and remained a reforming Anglican despite it, our work together ceased in 1970.

The Doctor believed that his summons to separation was a call for evangelical unity as such, and that he was not a denominationalist in any sense. In continuing to combat error, commend truth, and strengthen evangelical ministry as best I could in the Church of England, he thought I was showing myself a denominationalist and obstructing evangelical unity, besides being caught in a hopelessly compromised position. By contrast, I believed that the claims of evangelical unity do not require ecclesiastical separation where the faith is not actually being denied and renewal remains possible; that the action for which the Doctor called would be, in effect, the founding of a new, loose-knit, professedly undenominational denomination; and that he, rather than I, was the denominationalist for insisting that evangelicals must all belong to this new grouping and no other. His claim that this was what the times and the truth required did not convince me. Was either of us right? History will judge, and to history I remit the matter.

Born and reared in South Wales, he was fourteen in 1914 when his family moved to London. He entered the medical school of St. Bartholomew's Hospital at the early age of sixteen, graduated brilliantly in 1921, and soon became chief clinical assistant to his former teacher, the Royal Physician, Sir Thomas (later, Lord) Horder, an outstanding diagnostician whose analytical habit of mind reinforced his own. But he soon found that medical practice did not satisfy him, since it centered on the body while the deepest problems are in the soul. Having found his own way to an assurance of God's pardoning mercy towards him, he became sure that God was calling him to preach the gospel to others. By "gospel" he meant the old-fashioned, Bible-based, life-transforming message of radical sin in every human heart and radical salvation through faith in Christ alone—a definite message quite distinct from the indefinite hints and euphoric vaguenesses that to his mind had usurped the gospel's place in most British pulpits. In 1927, having decided that seminary training was not for him, he became lay pastor of the Forward Movement Mission Church of the Presbyterian (Calvinistic Methodist) Church of Wales in Sandfields, Aberavon, not far from Swansea. On his first Sunday as pastor he called for spiritual reality in terms so characteristic of his subsequent ministry that it is worth quoting his words at length.

"Young men and women, my one great attempt here at Aberavon, as long as God gives me strength to do so, will be to try to prove to you not merely that Christianity is reasonable, but that ultimately, faced as we all are at some time or other with the stupendous fact of life and death, nothing else is reasonable. That is, as I see it, the challenge of the gospel of Christ to the modern world. My thesis will ever be, that, face to face with the deeper questions of life and death, all our knowledge and our culture will fail us, and that our only hope of peace is to be found in the crucified Christ. . . . My request is this: that we all be honest with one another in our conversation and discussions. . . . Do let us be honest with one another and never profess to believe more than is actually true to our experience. Let us always, with the help of the Holy Spirit, testify to our belief, *in full*, but never a word more. . . . I do not know what your experience is, my friends, but as for myself, I shall feel much more ashamed to all eternity for the occasions on which I said I believed in Christ when in fact I did not, than for the occasions when I said honestly that I could not truthfully say that I did believe. If the church of Christ on earth could but get rid of the parasites who only believe that they ought to believe in Christ, she would, I am certain, count once more in the world as she did in her early days, and as she has always done during times of spiritual awakening. I ask you therefore tonight, and shall go on asking you and myself, the same question: Do you know what you know about the gospel? Do you question yourself about your belief and make sure of yourself?" (Iain H. Murray, *David Martyn Lloyd Jones: The First Forty Years, 1899-1939*, Edinburgh: Banner of Truth Trust, 1982, pp. 135 ff.).

"Prove"—"reasonable"—"modern world"—"honest"—"the crucified Christ"—"the help of the Holy Spirit"—"experience"—"spiritual awakening"—"question yourself"—these were keynote terms and phrases in the Doctor's preaching, first to last. He started as he meant to go on, and as he did in fact go on, seeing himself as an evangelist first and foremost and seeking constantly the conversion and quickening of folk in the churches who thought they were Christians already.

Though the Sandfields ministry was directed to working-class people, the intellectual challenge was always at its forefront. Social activities were scrapped, and with intense seriousness the Doctor gave himself to preaching and teaching the word of God. Soon he was ordained; the congregation grew, many conversions occurred, the church was admired as a model, and its minister was the best-known preacher in Wales.

In 1938 the Doctor moved to London's Congregational cathedral, Westminster Chapel, as colleague to the veteran G. Campbell Morgan. There, after Morgan's retirement in 1943, he was sole pastor for a quarter of a century, preaching morning and evening every Sunday save for his annual vacations in July and August. As in Wales, he lived at full stretch. Guest preaching during the first part of the week and pastoral counseling by appointment were regular parts of his life. On each Friday night he taught publicly at the Chapel, for fifteen years or so by discussion, then by doctrinal lectures, and for the last twelve years by exposition of Paul's Letter to the Romans. At both Sunday services, and on the Friday nights when Romans was explored, attendance was regularly nearer two thousand than one. In addition to his steady converting and nurturing ministry there, he exercised much influence on English evangelicalism as a whole.

He did a great deal to guide, stabilize, and deepen the evangelical student work of the young Inter-Varsity Fellowship of Evangelical Unions (IVF). At first he hesitated to touch IVF, for he was Welsh, middle-class, church-oriented, and intellectually and theologically alert, whereas IVF was a loose inter-denominational grouping that had grown out of children's and teenagers' ministry and was characterized by what the Doctor saw as brainless English upper-class pietism. But in partnership with another ex-medical man, the quiet genius Douglas Johnson, he fulfilled a leadership role in IVF for twenty years, and did more than anyone to give the movement its present temper of intellectual concern, confidence, and competence.

In due course the International Fellowship of Evangelical Students (IFES) was formed, an umbrella organization uniting student-led movements of IVF type all round the world. The Doctor drew up its basis, defined its platform, chaired its meetings for the first twelve years, and continued in association with it, first as president and then as vice-president, to the end of his life. In this, too, he was closely linked with the self-effacing Johnson, whose behind-the-scenes activity was a major factor in bringing IFES to birth.

Throughout his London years, the Doctor was also host and chairman of the Westminster Ministers' Fraternal (the Westminster Fellowship, as it was called), which met monthly at the Chapel for a day of discussion and mutual encouragement. Originally an idea of Johnson's, the Fraternal grew to a membership of 400 in the early 1960s. Through his masterful leadership of it, the Doctor focused its vision and shaped the ideals of many evangelical clergy in all denominations.

He campaigned steadily for the study of older evangelical literature, particularly the Puritans, Jonathan Edwards, and eighteenth and nineteenth-century biography, from which he had himself profited enormously. Also, he gave much support to the Banner of Truth Trust, a publishing house specializing in reprints, which was formed and financed from within his congregation. It can safely be said that the current widespread appreciation in Britain of older evangelical literature owes more to him than to anyone.

What a fascinating human being he was! Slightly built, with a great domed cranium, head thrust forward, a fighter's chin and a grim line to his mouth, he radiated resolution, determination, and an unwillingness to wait for ever. A very strong man, you would say, and you would be right. You can sense this from any photograph of him, for he never smiled into the camera. There was a touch of the old-fashioned about him: he wore linen collars, three-piece suits, and boots in public, spoke on occasion of crossing-sweepers and washerwomen, and led worship as worship was led a hundred years before his time. In the pulpit he was a lion, fierce on matters of principle, austere in his gravity, able in his prime both to growl and to roar as his argument required. Informally, however, he was a delightfully relaxed person, superb company, twinkling and witty to the last degree. His wit was as astringent as it was quick and could leave you feeling you had been licked by a cow. His answer to the question, posed in a ministers' meeting, "Why are there so few men in our churches?" was: "Because there are so many old women in our pulpits!" (Americans, please note: that was no reference to female preachers! In Britain an "old woman" is any dithery man without grip.) In 1952 he complained to me of the presence at the Puritan conference of two young ladies from his congregation. "They're only here for the men!" said he. "Well, Doctor," I replied, "as a matter of fact I'm going to marry one of them." (I had proposed and been accepted the night before.) I thought that would throw him, but it didn't at all. Quick as a flash came the answer: "Well, you see I was right about one of them; now what about the other?" There's repartee for you!

He did not suffer fools gladly and had a hundred ways of deflating pomposity. Honest, diffident people, however, found in him a warmth and friendliness that amazed them.

For he was a saint, a holy man of God: a naturally proud person whom God made humble; a naturally quick-tempered person to whom God taught patience; a naturally contentious person to whom God gave restraint and wisdom; a natural egoist, conscious of his own great ability, whom God set free from self-seeking to serve the servants of God. In his natural blend of intelligence with arrogance, quickness with dogmatism, and geniality with egocentricity, he was like two other small men who also wanted to see things changed, and spent their mature years changing them. The first, John Wesley, another great leader and encourager, just as shrewd and determined as the Doctor though less well-focused theologically, shaped a new, passionate style of piety for over a hundred thousand Englishmen in his own lifetime. The second, Richard Wagner, not a Christian, but a magnetic, emotional, commanding personality, charming, ingenious, well aware of his own powers, and very articulate (though muddily; not like the Doctor!), changed the course of Western music. The Doctor might not have appreciated either of these comparisons, but I think they are both in point. It is fascinating to observe what sort of goodness it is that each good man exhibits, and to try to see where it has come from. The Doctor was an intellectual like John Calvin, and like him said little about his inward experiences with God, but as with Calvin the moral effects of grace in his life were plain to see. His goodness, like Calvin's, had been distilled out of the raw material of a temperament inclined to pride, sharpness, and passion. Under the power of gospel truth, those inclinations had been largely mortified and replaced by habits of humility, good-will, and self-control. In public discussion he could be severe to the point of crushing, but always with transparent patience and good humor. I think he had a temper, but I never saw him lose it, though I saw stupid people "take him on" in discussion and provoke him in a manner almost beyond belief. His self-control was marvelous: only the grace of God suffices to explain it.

Beyond all question, the Doctor was brilliant: he had a mind like a razor, an almost infallible memory, staggering speed of thought, and total clarity and ease of speech, no matter what the subject or how new the notions he was voicing. His thinking always seemed to be far ahead of yours; he could run rings round anyone in debate; and it was hard not to treat him as an infallible oracle. However, a clever man only becomes a great one if two further qualities are added to his brilliance, namely, nobility of purpose and some real personal force in pursuing it. The Doctor manifested both these further qualities in an outstanding way.

He was essentially a preacher, and as a preacher primarily an evangelist. Some might question this since most of his twenty books (edited sermons, every one of them) have a nurturing thrust, and the quickening of Christians and churches was certainly the main burden of his final years of ministry. Also, his was supremely what Spurgeon called an "all-round" ministry, in practice as rich pastorally as it was evangelistically. But no one who ever heard him preach the gospel from the Gospels and show how it speaks to the aches and follies and nightmares of the modern heart will doubt that this was where his own focus was, and where as a communicator he was at his finest. He was bold enough to believe that because inspired preaching changes individuals it can change the church and thereby change the world, and the noble purpose of furthering such change was the whole of his life's agenda. As for force in pursuing his goal, the personal electricity of his pulpit communication was unique. All his energy went into his preaching: not only animal energy, of which he had a good deal, but also the God-given liveliness and authority that in past eras was called *unction*. He effectively proclaimed the greatness of God, and of Christ, and of the soul, and of eternity, and supremely of saving grace—the everlasting gospel, old yet ever new, familiar yet endlessly wonderful.

Unction is the anointing of God's Holy Spirit upon the preacher in and for his act of opening up God's written word. George Whitefield, who was in his own day the undisputed front-man of the evangelical awakening on both sides of the Atlantic, and whom the Doctor confessedly took as a role-model, once in conversation gave a printer *carte blanche* to transcribe and publish his sermons provided that he printed "the thunder and the lightning too"—but who could do that? In some way there was in the Doctor's preaching thunder and lightning that no tape or transcription ever did or could capture—power, I mean, to mediate a realization of God's presence (for when Whitefield spoke of thunder and lightning he was talking biblically, not histrionically, and so am I). Nearly forty years on, it still seems to me that all I have ever known about preaching was given me in the winter of 1948-49, when I worshiped at Westminster Chapel with some regularity. Through the thunder and lightning, I felt and saw as never before the glory of Christ and of his gospel as modern man's only lifeline and learned by experience why historic Protestantism looks on preaching as the supreme means of grace and of communion with God. Preaching, thus viewed and valued, was the center of the Doctor's life: into it he poured himself unstintingly; for it he pleaded untiringly. Rightly, he believed that preachers are born rather than made, and that preaching is caught more than it is taught, and that the best way to vindicate preaching is to preach. And preach he did, almost greedily, till the very end of his life— "this our short, uncertain life and earthly pilgrimage," as by constant repetition in his benedictions he had taught Christians to call it.

I mentioned thunder and lightning: that could give a wrong impression. Pulpit dramatics and rhetorical rhapsodies the Doctor despised and never indulged in; his concern was always with the flow of thought, and the emotion he expressed as he talked was simply the outward sign of passionate thinking. The style is the man, "the physiognomy of the mind," as Schopenhauer rather portentously said, and this was supremely true of the Doctor. He never put on any sort of act, but talked in exactly the same way from the pulpit, the lecture-desk, or the armchair, treating all without exception as fellow-enquirers after truth, who might or might not be behaving in character at just that moment. Always he spoke as a debater making a case (the Welsh are great debaters); as a physician making a diagnosis; as a theologian blessed with what he once recognized in another as a "naturally theological mind," thinking things out from scripture in terms of God; and as a man who loved history and its characters and had thought his way into the minds and motives, the insights and the follies, of very many of them.

He had read widely, thought deeply, and observed a great deal of human life with a clear and clinical eye, and as he was endlessly interested in his fellow-men, so he was a fascinating well of wisdom whenever he talked. When he preached, he usually eschewed the humor which bubbled out of him so naturally at other times and concentrated on serious, down-to-earth, educational exposition. He planned and paced his discourses (three-quarters of an hour or more) with evident care, never letting the argument move too fast for the ordinary listener and sometimes, in fact, working so hard in his first few minutes to engage his hearers' minds that he had difficulty getting the argument under way at all. But his preaching always took the form of an argument, biblical, evangelical, doctrinal and spiritual, starting most usually with the foolishness of human self-sufficiency, as expressed in some commonly held opinions and policies, moving to what may be called the Isaianic inversion whereby man who thinks himself great is shown to be small and God whom he treats as small is shown to be great, and always closing within sight of Christ—his cross and his grace. In his prime, when he came to the Isaianic inversion and the awesome and magnificent thing that he had to declare at that point about our glorious, self-vindicating God, the Doctor would let loose the thunder and lightning with a spiritual impact that was simply stunning. I have never known anyone whose speech communicated such a sense of the reality of God as did the Doctor in those occasional moments of emphasis and doxology. Most of the time, however, it was clear, steady analysis, reflection, correction and instruction, based on simple thoughts culled from the text, set out in good order with the minimum of extraneous illustration or decoration. He knew that God's way to the heart is through the mind (he often insisted that the first thing the gospel does to a man is to make him think), and he preached in a way designed to help people think and thereby grasp truth—and in the process be grasped by it, and so be grasped by the God whose truth it is.

A Welshman who inspired Englishmen, as David Lloyd-George once did on the political front; an eighteenth-century man (so he called himself) with his finger firmly on mid-twentieth century pulses; a preacher who could make "the old, old story of Jesus and his love" sound so momentously new that you felt you had never heard it before; a magisterial pastor and theologian whose only degrees were his medical qualifications; an erudite intellectual who always talked the language of the common man; a "Bible Calvinist" (as distinct from a "system Calvinist:" his phrase again) whose teaching all evangelicals could and did applaud; an evangelical who resolutely stood apart from the evangelical establishment, challenging its shallowness and short-sightedness constantly; a spiritual giant, just over five feet tall; throwback and prophet; loner and communicator; a compound of combative geniality, wisdom, and vision, plus a few endearing quirks—the Doctor was completely his own man, and quite unique.

On February 6, 1977, the fiftieth anniversary of the start of his ministry at Sandfields, the Doctor returned and preached. He announced as his text 1 Corinthians 2:2, "For I determined not to know any thing among you, save Jesus Christ, and him crucified." His sermon, printed in the *Evangelical Magazine of Wales*, in April 1981, the first issue following his death, began as follows:

"I have a number of reasons for calling your attention tonight to this particular statement. One of them—and I think you will forgive me for it—is that it was actually the text I preached on, on the first Sunday night I ever visited this Church . . .

"I call attention to it not merely for that reason, but rather because it is still my determination, it is still what I am endeavoring, as God helps me, to do. I preached on this text then—I have no idea what I said in detail, I have not got the notes—but I did so because it was an expression of my whole attitude towards life. It was what I felt was the commission that had been given to me. And I call attention to it again because it is still the same, and because I am profoundly convinced that this is what should control our every endeavour as Christian people and as members of the Christian Church at this present time."

There followed a very clear exposition of salvation through the atoning death of Jesus Christ, and then from the seventy-seven-year-old preacher came the application:

"Men and women, is Jesus Christ and him crucified everything to you? This is the question. It is a personal matter. Is he central? Does he come before anything and everything? Do you pin your faith in him and in him alone? Nothing else works. He works! I stand here because I can testify to the same thing. 'E'er since, by faith, I saw the stream / Thy flowing wounds supply, / Redeeming love has been my theme, / And shall be till I die.' 'God forbid that I should glory, save in the cross of our Lord Jesus Christ, by whom the world is crucified unto me, and I [crucified] unto the world'" (Gal 6:14).

"My dear friends, in the midst of life we are in death. This is not theory; this is personal, this is practical. How are you living? Are you happy? Are you satisfied? How do you face the future? Are you alarmed? Terrified? How do you face death? You have got to die. . . . What will you have when that end comes? You will have nothing, unless you have Jesus Christ and him crucified. . . . do you know him? Have you believed in him? Do you see that he alone can avail you in life, in death, and to all eternity? If not, make certain tonight. Fall at his feet. He will receive you, and he will make you a new man or a new woman. He will give you a new life. He will wash you. He will cleanse you. He will renovate you. He will regenerate you and you will become a saint, and you will follow after that glorious company of saints that have left this very place and are now basking in the sunshine of his face in the glory everlasting. Make certain of it, ere it be too late!"

Four years later, on the feast day of Wales' patron saint, the preacher himself was taken home. He died of cancer. He lies buried in the cemetery of the Phillips family, from which his wife came, in Newcastle Emlyn, near the farm which had belonged to his mother's people. The words, "For I determined not to know any thing among you, save Jesus Christ, and him crucified," are inscribed on his gravestone. Nothing more appropriate could be imagined.

"When nature removes a great man," said Emerson, "people explore the horizon for a successor, but none comes and none will. His class is extinguished with him." That is the case here. There is no one remotely resembling the Doctor around today, and we are the poorer as a result. To have known him was a supreme privilege, for which I shall always be thankful. His last message to his family, scribbled shakily on a notepad just before he died, when his voice had already gone, was: "Don't pray for healing; don't try to hold me back from the glory," and for me those last words, "the glory," point with precision to the significance that under God he had in my life. He embodied and expressed "the glory"—the glory of God, of Christ, of grace, of the gospel, of the Christian ministry, of humanness according to the new creation—more richly than any man I have ever known. No man can give another a greater gift than a vision of such glory as this. I am forever in his debt.

SEVEN

Philip E. Howard, Jr.

by Thomas Howard

S OMEWHERE IN A SCRAPBOOK I have a snapshot of my father which
I took with a box camera when I was a small boy. The picture
shows him standing perhaps twenty feet away, wearing an old
Stetson hat and a soft leather jacket, aiming a rifle.

His aim is at ninety degrees to the camera, off to stage-right, so to
speak. He was very punctilious about guns, and would never allow
us to aim so much as our index finger, let alone a toy pistol, at
someone. He inherited this outlook from his father and grandfather. His grandfather had had experience with revolvers in Texas
and New Mexico, in the days when that was serious business. An
enormous long-barreled blue steel revolver lay in a bottom drawer
of the highboy in my parents' bedroom, but there was never any
ammunition, and I think my father had had the hammer welded
shut. The pistol had belonged to his grandfather. I used to take it
out and handle it from time to time. It seemed to conjure a whole
world in which my father's origins lay, and which somehow
constituted his native land.

I do not mean that he, or his fathers, had come from the Wild

West. They were New Englanders. The rifle in my snapshot was actually a Daisy Red Rider air rifle which shot copper beebees by means of a spring mechanism. My father used to sting wandering dogs with these harmless rounds when they came onto the lawn with the clear intention of parking. He was kind to animals, but he did not want the lawn fouled.

These guns bespoke a world that was disappearing by the time I came along, and which is inaccessible and incomprehensible altogether to the generation now afoot. My son, for example, thinks of guns principally in connection with Viet Nam, the Mafia, 007 films, or drunken deer hunters in their pickup trucks.

My father's world was not a world of guns. But to see him settle the stock of that beebee rifle against his shoulder and squint through the sight was to see a man at home with certain suppositions about life. A good man and a gentleman may be trusted to know what firearms are for and to handle them with the skill and caution appropriate to such things. My father was justly proud of his marksmanship but had never fired a bullet at anything but a target. He was not a hunter. He took no pleasure in killing anything. But the notion that the way to prevent murder might be to enact laws banning all firearms would have struck him as insolent and maudlin. He and his generation would have objected that no murderer on earth will be deflected from his intentions for one moment by any such ban and that the people who plump for causes like this are themselves perhaps a threat to the sanity and continuity of civilization.

His was a world that counted on certain virtues and that saw these virtues as supporting the edifice of civility. Honor, courage, rectitude, courtesy: it was the responsibility of a good man and a gentleman to assist in protecting civility against all churlishness by embodying these things. My father was embarrassed and angered by any display, especially public, of churlishness. Indeed, it would not be going too far to say that any such display roused dread in him as well since, in the end, it will be churlishness that will bring down the edifice. Someone appearing in church or on a train dressed inappropriately; a couple nuzzling and billing in a public place; bad grammar, especially in print or from the podium; duck-tail haircuts and diamond pinkie rings on middle-aged men; lucite stiletto heels and painted toenails on women: these looked like fissures in the wall to my father.

He loved fly-fishing. His long, whiplike, split-bamboo fly rods could be dismantled into three sections. I used to like pulling them apart, listening to the small pop as the metal-sheathed butt of one section came out of the hollow metal sleeve at the tip of the next. He would set his equipment out neatly at the edge of the wide porch of our summer house in the White Mountains: the basket with the square hole in the top, lined with wet grass fresh from the meadow next to the house; the fat leather envelope with the flannel pages in it holding the flies—Dolly Vardens, Parmachenee Belles, Silver Doctors; extra leader, coiled in its round, flat tin box (the leader he would fix for me had tiny split-lead shot pinched onto it at intervals, for my worm fishing); his reel; the net; and his olive-drab hip boots, standing upright side by side, with the upper part of them fallen over sideways from the knee, the rubber belt-straps trailing on the porch floor. He always pinned his fishing license to the band of his old Stetson hat.

If he were setting out to fish down one of the little brooks that come off the mountains up there, this was all he needed. If he were headed for a lake, he would put the canoe on the top of the car. He was a fine canoeist and had taught all of his children about the little flick you give to the stern paddle to keep the canoe from weaving back and forth in the water. To this day the first thing I look for when I see someone out in a canoe is whether they know how to do this or not. Almost no one does. My father felt that it is a great pity for people to have so little idea about what an exquisite thing a canoe is. They ought not to be out there, really. Let them flounder about in rowboats if they want to. Aluminum canoes, and Sponson canoes with the air chambers along the gunwales to keep them from tipping over, struck my father as betraying the grace that belongs to the idea of canoes. A canoe is made of canvas.

He would sometimes take me fishing with him. He taught all of his children as much about fishing as they wanted to learn. Two of my brothers became good fly fishermen. I never went beyond worms, but I learned very early that fly fishing is the finest sport there is.

My father would stand in the brook with the water rushing past his boots, just a little upstream from some nice hole under a big rock. He knew the habits and wisdom of trout and saw his fishing as a gentlemanly contest of wits with them. Native brook and rainbow trout were the most elegant fish in the world, in his view. Pickerel, pike, bass, perch, and the rest of them, lacked the grace of trout. Hatchery trout were becoming a melancholy necessity in a world where too many people were turning out to fish.

He would play out the line with his left hand, pulling it in length after length from the reel, which clicked quietly as it spun. His right hand waved the rod forward and back with the line sailing in a great S-shape in the air. You could not tell where the thin bamboo ended and the line began. When he was satisfied that he had exactly the right length of line out, he would let the fly alight on the surface of the pool, right above the nose of the trout that was lurking under the rock. He would show me how to do all of this without whipping the line. If you whipped it, you could snap the leader and flies right off and lose them.

When a trout would strike at the fly, all of my father's powers would gather and poise in the blissful, delicate, and taxing game of landing it. The tip of the rod would flicker, bob, then plunge sharply down in a deep arc. With a deft movement of his wrist he would snare the trout, then reel in the line, seeing to it that no slack allowed the trout room for maneuver. There was always a breathless moment while he reached gingerly forward with the net in his left hand and dipped down under the thrashing trout. Not until the fish lay curved in the bottom of the net were you sure you had it.

"It's a rainbow," or "It's a brook," he would call as he waded to the bank.

My father did not like to leave a fish gasping slowly to death in the basket, so he would show me how to grasp it, insert a thumb into one of the gills, and with a quick pressure snap the spine just back of the fish's eye. The struggle was over in an instant.

Back at the house at the end of the day he would lay the catch out to be cleaned, side by side along a board, arranging them by size. Most of them would be brook trout, about eight inches long, with rosy spots along their smooth black sides. If the array were crowned with a fat, ten-inch native rainbow with the faint pink stripe along its silvery side, this was the best prize. You knew the meat would be pink.

With his tiny bone-handled penknife he would cut off the heads of the trout and slit the belly from the tail to the gills. Sometimes there would be roe among the viscera, and he always felt bad about that. A mother. He would scrape the inside immaculately clean under the faucet which stood next to the porch, showing us how to get the last black bits of blood from along the spine. A good fisherman will leave no trace of blood here. There was always a hint of ceremony as he arranged the clean trout on a blue-rimmed, white enamelled tin plate and set it on top of the great blocks of ice in the wooden ice box on the back porch. The door to the ice compartment would shut with a thick click. Trout for breakfast tomorrow.

I would awake the next morning in my third-floor room to bright sunshine and the racket of crows in the white pines in the meadow across the road. Sometimes I could hear a crackling from downstairs: this meant that my father thought the morning was snappy enough to warrant a fire in the enormous fireplace. Through the open window I could hear my mother, in the kitchen-house below, getting breakfast.

My father had taught her how to cook trout. You dip them in egg and cornmeal before you fry them. He taught us all how to eat them. You lay the trout on its back (not its side) on the plate with the tail towards you, steadying it by placing the tip of your knife between the two fat sides, just touching the backbone. With the tines of your fork pressing gently on the meat, you gradually lay the left side of the trout flat, leaving the whole ladder of tiny, filament-like bones still attached to the backbone, separated now from the meat. You do the same with the right side. Now lift the backbone and tail away from the trout altogether. Brush the meat with a pat of butter and sprinkle it lightly with salt and pepper. This is how it is done. Very few people and no restaurants at all know about this. Once or twice in my adult life I have ventured to order trout from a menu, hoping that I might recapture some fugitive memory of those breakfasts. My hopes have been ill-placed: the best fish that the best restaurant can set out seems cardboard next to the light, custardy delicacy of the trout that my father caught for us.

He was a great ornithologist as well as a fly-fisherman. Once or twice a year he would take us for bird-hikes. His favorite birds were the ones that lived in the White Mountains: the hermit thrush, the olive-sided flycatcher, the veery, the winter wren, the white-throated sparrow, and the black-capped chickadee. He could imitate flawlessly the songs of dozens of species and would get them to come and flit from twig to twig over his head, answering his calls. It troubled me somewhat, since I thought they might be saddened when no mate showed up. He always carried his "Peterson" (*A Field Guide to the Birds*), a checklist, and a pair of six-power binoculars hung around his neck on a thong. He rarely needed to consult Peterson, but there are some warblers which always require looking up.

He taught us to walk along in the fields and woods quietly, mainly remembering not to make any sudden gesture with our hands. It was sudden movements more than noises that frightened the birds, he said. When he spotted a bird he would raise his binoculars very slowly to his eyes. This would push the front brim of his Stetson up, changing his appearance quite remarkably. Comedians wore their hats this way, but comedy was not at all the note being struck here.

To hear a bird, locate its whereabouts, call it, spot it, name it, and let us have a look through the binoculars: this was his pleasure. Vesper sparrow; chewink; pine siskin; Lapland longspur; yellow-breasted chat; snow bunting; dickcissel; prothonotary warbler; parula warbler; loggerhead shrike; blue-gray gnatcatcher; long-billed marshwren; brown creeper; wood pewee: the names arouse fathomless nostalgia in me. And all the hawks: duck hawks, marsh hawks, Cooper's, rough-legged, red-tailed, sharp-shinned, broad-winged, and ospreys. And the owls: long-eared, barred, barn, screech, saw-whet, Richardson's, burrowing.

In the winter he would take us to the marshes in southern New Jersey, and to a sandy region known as the Pine Barrens, and to Barnegat Lighthouse on Long Beach Island, a thin, twenty-mile strip of sand off the coast. Here we hoped to see snowy owls, knots, sanderlings, curlews, ruddy turnstones, willets, godwits, semi-palmated plovers, oystercatchers, stilts, clapper rails, black-crowned night herons, and all kinds of teals, shovelers, mergansers, oldsquaws, scaup ducks, buffleheads, and grebes.

After we had had a good look at a bird, or at a flock of them, he would take from his pocket the stiff card on which the checklist was printed and draw a small dash in the margin next to the name of the species. He used Autopoint pencils with very soft black lead, which he would buy at a shop called Pomerantz, on Chestnut Street in Philadelphia. As I type this manuscript I am using an Autopoint with soft black lead to make my corrections and changes with. It is the best pencil in the world, and along with trout and birds, forms part of my father's legacy to me.

He loved hiking. There were half a dozen trails in the mountains around Franconia to which he returned, year after year, for more than fifty years. The Greenleaf Trail and the Bridle path, up Lafayette; the Lonesome Lake Trail; the Jewell Trail up Washington; and the Kinsman Flume and Bridal Veil Falls trails: these were his favorites, and he never seemed to tire of repeating them. There was a cluster of peeled walking sticks under the stairs in our summer house, and he would get these out and distribute them to us according to our height. There were also three or four small, flat, square packs which he called haversacks, made of extremely heavy khaki canvas, which my mother would fill with sandwiches, little red boxes of Sun-Maid raisins, Hershey bars (for energy), and "hermits"—soft, cake-like, gingery cookies. On the day of a hike we would always be awakened earlier than usual so that we could have a hearty breakfast and an early start. Early starts were part of the fabric of my father's world.

My mother would drive us to the base of the mountain to be climbed. Here the ritual was always the same: shoelaces were checked, haversack straps adjusted and settled comfortably on your shoulders, windbreaker jackets tied around your waist by knotting the sleeves in front. You gave your walking stick a last few prods into the ground to make sure it was the right length. Even though it was August, you could see your breath, and the long grass and ferns at the opening of the trail were still silver with dew and cobwebs.

Usually the trail dipped down and crossed a brook before it started to climb. There were always black-capped chickadees flitting about in the birch and maple trees overhead, with their churring "chicka-dee-dee-dee" call or their fife-like two-note song. My father had a certain gait for mountain climbing—a slow, steady plod, with his hands clasped behind him. He told us that if you start out scampering you will soon run out of breath. This steady gait will serve you well, hour after hour. On the upper slopes above the timberline, when the sun is hot and you have been climbing for several hours, you will still be going at the same pace.

In the first half-hour or so, when you were still walking along under the hardwood trees, he would point out the bunch-berries, clintonia borealis (there seemed to be no English name for this plant with the long single stalk and one shiny, dark blue berry), and moose maple. He told us that the enormous moose maple leaves would always serve as a useful substitute if you had forgotten to bring along tissues in your pack.

Further up you began to see Labrador tea and creeping snowberry next to the trail, and the hardwoods gave way gradually to spruce trees. A few tall straight ones would appear among the birches and maples; then the hardwoods disappeared and on either side of the path there would be dense growth of scrubby, gnarled spruces, their immemorial roots grasping the moss-covered rocks like tough old fingers that had been holding on against winds and blizzards since the beginning of the world. My father would take out his penknife and cut off little deposits of spruce gum that had oozed through the lichen-covered bark and give them to us to chew. You felt that this was a much cleaner and healthier confection than Wrigley's or Dentyne. It was certainly more astringent and less sugary.

As the trail climbed higher the trees grew stubbier and stubbier, until suddenly you found yourself at the timber line. Often a single step would take you from the scrubby spruce growth out into the immense upland above the timber line, with the whole world spreading away from you.

Now you could see the trail itself, following the cairns in a zigzag track all the way to the summit, and hundreds of peaks stretching away into Vermont and Canada. The song of the white-throated sparrows came like a crystal echo up from the spruce forest below, and from the clumps of grass between the boulders scattered across the upper reaches of the mountainside. You could also hear a tiny, infinitely high "pink-pink" from some bird whose name I have forgotten. My father would call back and forth to the white-throats, and would stop every few minutes just to sniff the air and gaze, with his hands on his hips. On most trips he would observe at least once that the scene here was a very long way from Thirteenth and Wood, the dingy corner in Philadelphia where his office was.

On Mt. Washington, he did not mind the somewhat quaint chuffing of the Cog Railway, which looked for all the world like something out of a children's storybook. But it was very hard for him to conceal his dismay over the passengers who alighted at the summit, with their rope-soled shoes, Bermuda shorts, slant-eyed sunglasses, cameras, and Hawaiian sports shirts. They knew nothing about mountains, he felt. The summit was being wasted on this crowd who had no ears for the song of the white-throat. They came and pawed over the decals and ashtrays and bawdy farmyard postcards in the souvenir shop, then reboarded the train for the Base Station. To my father, their faces seemed jelled in expressions of ennui, surfeit, and confusion.

For most of the year, my father was a commuter. We lived in Moorestown, New Jersey, which had been settled by Philadelphia Quakers. When I was a small boy, the air of the town was still redolent of Quakerism: broad, quiet streets richly shaded by huge oaks, elms, and maples; large comfortable houses; and people greeting each other with nods, cheery smiles, and twinkly eyes that seemed full of old Philadelphia. "Good morning, Philip Howard, how is thee?" or "Good morning, Kathy dear, how's thee today?" I would hear them say to my parents. We were not Quakers, but my parents spoke the "plain language" with their Quaker friends.

Moorestown lay about ten miles from Philadelphia, across the Delaware River. A single track of the Pennsylvania Railroad came through the town, connecting Philadelphia with Atlantic City. There were steam engines in those days, and the passenger coaches were painted a dull brick-color. My father very much liked the ride into town (he always said "in town" when he referred to Philadelphia), since it gave him an unbroken thirty minutes or so to read. He would leave the house at 7:40 A.M. and walk the few blocks to the station, allowing himself the exact number of minutes to get there. There was never the smallest flurry. After breakfast and family prayers, which were timed so that none of us ever needed to race about hunting for school books and finishing up chores, he would go to the hall closet, put his maroon wool scarf around his neck, pinning it down with his chin as he put on his overcoat. Then his hat and gloves. He would pick up his briefcase, kiss my mother good-bye, tipping his hat back as he did so, and go out the door. His briefcase was a soft leather affair with straps that buckled. He had a certain way of flipping the straps back when he undid the buckles.

My father's professional life was familiar to all of his children, since we would often find ourselves in town for one reason or another, and this almost always included a visit to "the office." He was the editor of a weekly religious journal called *The Sunday School Times*, which had a very large readership all over the world. It was looked upon as an almost infallibly trustworthy court of appeal by hundreds of thousands of Protestants. The weight of responsibility which my father felt in this connection was almost insupportable to him and was made even more onerous by the fact that his uncle before him, and his grandfather before that, had been the only other editors in the century of the journal's existence. I grew up with the unconscious assumption that a man's adult responsibilities would doubtless crush him in the end. The "problems in the office" which we heard him talk about with my mother ranged from appalling ecclesiastical wars on which he was obliged, reluctantly, to adopt some official editorial point of view, to falling circulation, to quarreling and tears among "the girls in the office." This last problem contributed far more to the deep creases in his face and the gray in his hair than did the official matters.

The girls in the office were the secretaries, accountants, and proofreaders. Most of them were aging. Indeed, to my ten-year-old eyes, they all seemed to be very old women. They always greeted us with delighted shrieks and little favors when we came into the office; but we knew that they brought on our father's greatest agonies. He had neither the disposition nor the ability to cope with what would now be called "interpersonal relationships"—a phrase that would have given him worse pains than the quarrels themselves. But he felt that the whole atmosphere in the office depended on him personally. The sight of one of these women sniffing into her hanky and mopping reddened eyes filled him with more dread and vexation than almost anything else in the world.

The offices of this journal occupied the sixth floor of a factory building. Spaces had been created for the different departments by arranging dark-green metal bookcases into corridors and squares. A few paper-thin wooden partitions had been set up for the more important offices. My father had one of these. It was a small, cold, corner cubicle with enormous factory windows overlooking the morgue. I would prop open one of the metal-rimmed window sections and crane my head through it, fascinated with horror if a hearse drew up below. Once I saw them fling the stiffened, emaciated, stark-naked body of a man from the hearse onto the loading platform. Occasionally the air was heavy with a strange, sweet smoke.

I have, somewhere, another snapshot of my father at his desk in this office. He is sitting there, tall and straight, with his gold chain and Phi Beta Kappa key across the front of his vest. This key was the one concession that he made to anything that might at all be called vanity. My impression is that the question arose in his mind from time to time as to whether it might not, in fact, be vain for a man to display his Phi Beta Kappa key. But somehow or other he found room in his otherwise remorseless moral categories to go on wearing it. On one end of the chain there was some arrangement to keep the end in one of the vest pockets. On the other end, in the other pocket, was his gold Longines watch, thin as an after-dinner mint. This watch kept flawless time, decade after decade. He would check it once a week at a chronometer that sat in the window of a jeweler's on Walnut Street. He would show us this chronometer when he took us out to lunch on the days when we visited him in the office.

He usually ate lunch alone. If he had to entertain someone, he would arrange to meet them at the Whittier Hotel, which had a quiet dining room with starched white tablecloths. Otherwise he would leave the office and walk, with his very long strides, five or six blocks along Thirteenth Street to his favorite restaurant, a cafeteria called The Colonnade. It was in an arcade that opened off one of the small streets—Sansom or Juniper—near City Hall. You had to go down some stairs to get to this place. My memory of it is of a tiled floor, a great many mirrors and brass rails, and hundreds of small tables with bentwood chairs at them. The place was always crowded, but things moved so fast that there was never any trouble getting a table. Someone was always leaving.

My father liked The Colonnade because you could get plain, well-cooked food without wasting any time at all. He also liked the walk to and from his office. He rarely used the elevator on his comings and goings from the building. The trip up and down the six flights of stairs to his office was good for a man, he felt.

The desk where my father sits in my snapshot has no clutter on it. It never did. Any letter or manuscript on which he was not working at the moment lay in either the In or the Out box. There was a small marble rack on the desk with grooves, in which lay his pencils. He always carried a black Esterbrook fountain pen with an extra broad nib in his upper vest pocket. He used this to sign his name. Otherwise he worked with pencils.

He did all of his correspondence and writing on an Ediphone, which even in those days was an outdated model. It sat up on a little metal cart like a tea tray, with casters on the legs so that you could push it around. There were wax cylinders and a mouthpiece like a small horn at the end of a snakelike metal arm that had sections like little vertebrae to make it flexible. My father would tilt the upper edge of the mouthpiece against his upper lip and talk into it. He always included exact typing instructions in what he said. I would sometimes listen to him dictate and would hear "... Comma. Quote. Cap.," or "Paren. Point. Paragraph." He knew everything there was to know about editing, printing, proofreading, and prose. His own prose style was as flawless as the foundations of the City of God. It was without the smallest embellishment and perfect in its economy and integrity. He did not like polysyllables, elaborate metaphors, circumlocution, fustian, pyrotechnics, or any suggestion of self-display in prose (he would have drawn a single blue line through this sentence).

Every week he had to write an "Ed. Note." These were short essays, perhaps 300 words long, which appeared in a double column in the upper right-hand section of the front page. He enjoyed writing these pieces. The discipline of saying something helpful, clear, and substantial in such a short space kept his mind and his prose lean. He always had the simplest reader in mind as he wrote, and he usually drew some illustration of his point from ordinary life. Often his love for birds, fishing, and the mountains would appear, but only reticently and briefly, and never by way of displaying his personal hobbies or knowledge.

These editorial notes invariably had for their main burden some direct point from the Bible. He never pontificated about public issues. The world changes very little, in his view, from aeon to aeon. Hence very little is to be gained by raising the hue and cry about some new outrage, as though here were something that had caught us all off guard and about which we must become scandalized and take up arms. He had traditional political, economic, and social views, and hence it depressed him to watch Franklin Roosevelt win election after election. But he spent very little time worrying over the enfeebling effect that liberalism has on civilization: he assumed that all civilizations are transitory and that most palaces and chancellories have been mare's nests of intrigue since the beginning of time. I never heard him puff and blow about corrupt political machinery, even though he was aware of it all, and it depressed him. By the same token, he rarely talked and never wrote, so far as I know, about Hitler, even though he, like all good men, was paralyzed with horror at the huge rallies in Nuremberg, and, later, at the revelations from Treblinka and Belsen.

We had an American flag leaning out from a bracket on the front porch railing at home during World War II, and, when my oldest brother went into the Army, we hung in a window the small red-bordered, white silk square with the blue star in the middle. My father was impressed and moved by military parades, not because the brisk, unison thud of martial heels roused a cheap jingoism in him, but because here came the flag, supported and attended by men who might die to preserve the gentlest kind of life ever offered to a people by a society.

The spectacle of military precision thrilled him. Strapping MPs with glistening boots, starched khakis, white gloves, and glossy helmet liners worn smartly forward almost touching the bridge of the nose; glittering jeeps and staff cars wheeling up with perfect timing and in perfect formation with little flags standing up stiffly from the front fenders; the long, harsh yell of sergeants-major snapping thousands of men from parade rest to attention without the slightest possibility of disorder, unrest, or protest. I think my father glimpsed in all of this the order that arches over things and that alone can shelter the gentility and civility that should mark human life. It all stood at a polar extreme from the slovenliness, egoism, truculence, and indulgence that deface life and make a ruin of it.

But public life and issues were not where my father's imagination dwelt. He believed that if a man studied the Bible sedulously, every day of his life, he would be in touch with the only finally enduring wisdom there is. Something like this seems to be very much the burden of the Book of Proverbs, and of Psalm 119, and, in some sense, of Christ's words about man not living by bread alone. My father had a very earnest, and very direct and personal, devotion to the Bible. This was apparent in the Ed. Notes that he wrote every week. He did his best in these short columns to lodge simple scriptural teachings in people's minds.

Certainly his favorite theme was trust. This was ironic, since he himself did not manage to reach anything like serenity until the last five years of his life. He was greatly burdened with life and its responsibilities. But he hung onto such texts as "Trust ye in the Lord forever, for in the Lord Jehovah is everlasting strength," and "What time I am afraid, I will trust in thee," and "Casting all your care upon him, for he careth for you." He wrote about this theme perpetually.

He himself studied the Bible most earnestly every day of his life, and in so far as he ever permitted himself to suppose that he might have any "ministry," I think he would have ventured to hope that he might be instrumental in pointing others straight to the pages of the Bible. He felt that Protestant modernism, arising as it did from the twin springs of nineteenth-century evolutionary optimism and of German biblical criticism, had perpetrated a monstrous and tragic fraud on people by robbing them of the Bible. Somehow the churchgoing public had been given to believe that Christianity was mainly a matter of everyone's endeavoring to cultivate amiable thoughts and support progressive social movements. Where was the miraculous? my father wondered. Where was sin? Where were the ancient doctrines of atonement, regeneration, sanctification, and judgment? Where, in this pallid and vitiated religion, was the individual Christian with his Bible and his daily fervent walk with God?

My father never attacked anyone in his writings. But he, along with the early Fundamentalists, tried to keep the ancient faith intact. He found himself, thus, in very odd company at times. Doctrinally he had cast his lot with these Fundamentalists; and the men who stood at the sources of the movement were congenial enough to him for the most part, since they shared not only his unabashedly traditional faith, but also his sensibilities. They, like him, had come from the old universities. Many of them were Presbyterians, as he was. Many were Philadelphians. As such, they were civilized men.

But the gospel, when it is preached in all of its apostolic simplicity, will not stay inside any such circle. It has a peculiar appeal to all sorts and conditions of men. My father found himself thrust into circles that he might not have picked had he been consulting only his own inclinations and frame of mind. But never once did I hear from him so much as a hint of anything that might at all be called condescension. He would not have known how to patronize. It certainly never occurred to him to reserve the smallest corner of his imagination as a kind of shrine where he could pay secret homage to his lineage, his breeding, his credentials, his education, or his sensibilities. He had neither the self-consciousness necessary for this sort of thing, nor any interest in it.

On the other hand, he reveled in his family. His mother's name was Trumbull, a name of some dignity in Hartford, and he had an array of Trumbull aunts, like duchesses from Trollope, who would come to our house for family gatherings. One of them actually did look something like the duchess in *Alice in Wonderland.* These aunts were not Fundamentalists, and I was never sure just where they might wish to locate themselves with respect to Christian notions. Their thin legs, pointy shoes with straps across the instep, complicated tangles of necklaces and pince-nez chains, soft-piled grey hair, freckled and blue-veined hands, and rings that slipped around under their fingers so that the stones were always underneath: this was what my father had come from, in my eyes. The Trumbulls were violent, imperial, and droll. They were all great raconteurs, exulting in scandalous exaggeration. My great-aunts had high, rich voices with that intermittent small, scrapy break in them that bespoke, I thought, a breeding fathomless in its impeccability and an aristocracy almost olympian in its serenity.

My father had inherited the drollery of these Trumbulls. It made its appearance in him, not so much in wild exaggerations as in a wry, dry, understated wit that was at its best when he was telling of his own misfortunes. Once when he was bent over a small suitcase that had very tightly sprung clasps that flew up as you undid them, he exclaimed, with feigned vexation, "Say! Every time I open this thing I flay my thumb knuckles!" He knew that there was nothing in the world that made us all laugh more than the apt use of a word. Another time he moved away from a roaring fire in the fireplace with, "Say! This fire has nearly burned the nap off my suit!" Once, late at night, when my mother objected to a small pile of clothes that he had placed in a corner of their bedroom, to be put in the hamper next morning, he countered with, "Why? Do you think some lethal miasma will arise from them all night long?"

He was a pied piper with children. He had a small repertoire of tricks that he could do, and would often collect around himself a semicircle of rapt grandchildren or neighborhood tots, and regale them. He could "swallow" his penknife, for example, then pull it out of a child's ear. Or he would create an appalling little face using a handkerchief, his fist, and two matches for the eyes. He had worked up a miniature rhythmic tattoo by snapping his fingers and popping his open left hand against the hollow of his loosely clenched right hand. This always kept children mesmerized, and you would see them going away fiddling with their fingers, trying to get the effect. He had also composed a four-line tune which he named "The Burlington County March," which he would play on the piano for anyone's delectation. He would get any assembled children to march in a file around the pattern at the edge of our living room rug, in time to his tune.

But all the self-assuredness of the Trumbulls had been left out of his makeup. This is difficult to account for, if we are thinking of heredity alone, since his father, on the other side, was an immensely strong, serene, apparently uncomplicated man. I knew him only when he was an old man; but he seems to me to have been the most perfectly civilized man I have ever known. The whole world of New England and Philadelphia stood before you when you met him; and yet he was without the slightest trace of self-importance. His laugh was hearty without being the bore that so many hearty laughs are, and he was at home and delighted, apparently in almost any company. His attitude towards small children was completely natural. He did not try to gear himself down to some supposed children's level of things for you: he took you into his world, quite without affectation.

Next to this family heritage, I think it was my father's reading which often lay between him and the company of religious allies among whom he found himself. Besides the general fare of English literature which he had had to read as a young man at Haverford College and the University of Pennsylvania, there were a few minor writers whose prose seemed to appeal to him. I remember hearing him talk about Ambrose Bierce and Joseph C. Lincoln. He also liked James Whitcomb Riley, and would quote "When the frost is on the punkin" from time to time, and "The Raggedy Man," who "had two eyes like two fried eggs, and a nose like a Bartlett pear."

But his real home when it came to books was to be found among such works as Philip Doddridge's *The Rise and Progress of Religion in the Soul,* William Law's *A Serious Call to a Devout and Holy Life,* Jeremy Taylor's *The Rule and Exercises of Holy Living,* and Richard Baxter's *A Call to the Unconverted* and *The Saints' Everlasting Rest.* These, with Bunyan, Luther on Galatians, and John Wesley's *Journals,* were the works he mentioned, and read, most often. The Bible commentaries he used were Matthew Henry and Conybeare and Howsen.

Hence, he was very far from being at ease with the somewhat tatterdemalion set of sensibilities that eventually came to accompany Fundamentalist piety. Chattiness and rickety syntax in public prayers; pert or sentimental expressions of devotion in hymnody, or worse, rhapsodic protestations of self-consecration to God; flashy showmanship in evangelistic meetings; and the apparently *ad hoc* nature of a great deal of what went on in church services: these filled my father with anguished embarrassment.

He was looked to as a leader, however, and hence often found himself on the platform as a speaker. I can remember looking at him from the congregation at meetings and conferences, sitting on the platform as he was being introduced. He would endure the introduction, and, when the moment came, uncoil his lean, six-foot-three-inch frame and approach the podium. To my young eyes, he seemed almost paralyzed by awkwardness at these moments. But looking back now over the distance of almost fifty years, I would say that what one saw was the reticence and self-deprecation of a man who wished most earnestly to say something true, clear, and helpful to a miscellaneous gathering of people who represented all sorts of backgrounds.

It would be a great mistake to think of anything highbrow in connection with my father. Whatever his family and education and taste meant in shaping his approach to things, it had not made a highbrow of him. This will have been clear to readers already with my mention of James Whitcomb Riley. The only "classical" music which I ever heard him whistle was a piece called "Liebesfreude" which he knew from a recording of Fritz Kreisler.

His entirely unsophisticated simplicity showed itself in his taste in hymns. He loved, first of all, the hymns of Wesley, Cowper, and Newton. He would sing "When All Thy Mercies, O My God," while he was shaving at the mirror in the morning, and the hymn which he usually whistled was "There Is a Fountain Filled with Blood." He would often stop at the piano for a few minutes and play two or three hymns. Usually these were the Gospel hymns, "Praise Him, Praise Him, Jesus Our Blessed Redeemer," and "All the Way My Saviour Leads Me," and "I Will Sing the Wondrous Story," and "Sing Them Over Again to Me, Wonderful Words of Life." When we were small, he would sing to us "I Think When I Read That Sweet Story of Old," and "Jesus, Keep Me Near the Cross." Somewhere in mid-life he discovered, in a Plymouth Brethren hymnal, the Swedish hymn, "If I Gained the World but Lost the Saviour," and this immediately became a favorite of his, both its words and its tune.

His happiness and contentment at home with my mother and the six of us children was such that he really did not want anything else out of life at all. Once in a while he indulged patently fanciful notions of trout fishing in New Zealand "someday." But otherwise he wanted to be at home. He liked the idea that we were a well-traveled family, but he did not actually like traveling, especially if this meant going away alone for a speaking engagement. He was on the board of trustees of a college in Illinois, and he enjoyed his once- or twice-yearly trips from Philadelphia to Chicago in a roomette on the Broadway Limited. The isolation and quiet for reading, and the rocking of the train as it shot through Pennsylvania in the darkness, pleased him. He had very much loved the transatlantic crossings he had made on shipboard and was vastly impressed with his first flight, and even more so with his first jet flight. These feats of technology and power roused the same sort of admiration in him as did military parades. But he had no hankering for tourism and sightseeing.

His love for my mother was almost schoolboyish. I saw him vexed, impatient, or angry with many things over the years; but never once did I ever see him treat my mother, or speak to her, with anything other than tenderness and affection. He would come into the kitchen while she was standing at the stove or the sink and put his arms around her from behind. He admitted to us that he liked the songs "Roamin' in the Gloamin'" and "The Sunshine of Your Smile," because they took him back to the days of their courtship.

Next to the Bible, his love for my mother, and his delight in his children, his greatest consolation in life was an orderly schedule. He got up at 5:00 A.M. daily for forty-five years, as far as I know, and spent the first hour of the day in his study, reading his Bible and praying. In cold weather he always wore a heavy woolen wrapper, and if you saw him before he had come back upstairs to shave, wash, and dress, two things struck you. First, his hair, which he parted in the middle and kept very short, was ungroomed. He always massaged Wildroot into it and brushed it back with two hairbrushes. This gave him a whole different look from the dry, early-morning look. Second, he had not yet put in his glass eye for the day, so his left eye, which stayed shut when the eye was not in it, looked flat. It was not as odd as an outsider might think, and he never made anything of the rather bizarre business of taking out the eye at night and putting it in again in the morning. It was only the work of a few seconds, and his children, growing up with it, hardly thought about it either. He had lost the eye in a Fourth of July accident when he was twelve. The artificial eye was cup-shaped, not spherical, and he kept it in a small leather box lined with chamois. When it was in the socket you could not tell one eye from the other.

His daily schedule followed, without stress, from this early start, timed down to the minute. Like his clear prose, his clean desk top, his neatly arrayed fishing equipment, the military spectacles that thrilled him, the wholesome simplicity of The Colonnade, the safety of his roomette on The Broadway Limited, the well-laid-out streets of Moorestown, and his direct, biblical faith tutored by a moderate Philadelphia Presbyterianism, an exact daily routine bespoke a well-ordered world. Short of heaven itself, which he longed for quite unashamedly, this is what he prized more than anything else, as the setting for life—his own life and the lives of his wife, his children, his friends, and indeed of all men.

EIGHT

Blaise Pascal

by Robert E. Coleman

IN THE YEAR OF GRACE, 1654,

On Monday, 23d of November, Feast of St. Clement, Pope and
Martyr, and of others in the Martyrology,
   Vigil of St. Chrysogonus, Martyr, and others, From about half
past ten in the evening until about half past twelve,

FIRE

God of Abraham, God of Isaac, God of Jacob,
not of the philosophers and scholars.
Certitude. Certitude. Feeling. Joy. Peace.
God of Jesus Christ.
"Thy God shall be my God."
Forgetfulness of the world and of everything, except God.
   He is to be found only by the ways taught in the Gospel.
   Greatness of the Human Soul.
   "Righteous Father, the world hath not known Thee, but I
have known Thee."

Joy, joy, joy, tears of joy.
I have separated myself from Him.
"My God, wilt Thou leave me?"
Let me not be separated from Him eternally.
"This is the eternal life, that they might know Thee, the only true God, and the one whom Thou hast sent, Jesus Christ."
Jesus Christ.

JESUS CHRIST

I have separated myself from Him: I have fled from Him, denied Him, crucified Him.
Let me never be separated from Him.
We keep hold of Him only by the ways taught in the Gospel.

Renunciation, total and sweet.
Total submission to Jesus Christ and to my director.
Eternally in joy for a day's training on earth. Amen.*

Seldom has one expressed with such precision and feeling his confrontation with Jesus Christ. The terse stenographic account was written on a parchment, at the top of which was etched a cross surrounded by rays. As a constant reminder of this experience, the paper was sewed by the author inside the lining of his coat. One can imagine him during times of temptation and suffering slipping his hand over the hidden treasure and pressing its hallowed message to his heart. Not until after his death was the document discovered. The reality which it describes changed the life of Blaise Pascal, universally acclaimed scientist, inventor, psychologist, philosopher, and Christian apologist; by any comparison one of the greatest thinkers of all time.

I was introduced to him while a graduate student at Princeton Theological Seminary. Dr. Emile Cailliet, a professor whose

---

* Blaise Pascal "Memorial" in *Great Shorter Works of Pascal,* translated by Emile Cailliet and John C. Blankenage (Philadelphia: Westminster Press, 1948), p. 117.

academic renown had not diminished his fervency of spirit, spoke so endearingly of Pascal that I was constrained to look into his life and work. The more I read, and the more deeply I read, the more I was captivated and challenged by his thought.

What insight to the reality of God! Here was a man without rival in intellectual attainment, yet possessing childlike simplicity of faith. I realized that I could learn a great deal from him. During these intervening years, the writings of Pascal have been close by my side.

He was born in Clermont-Ferrand in France, June 19, 1623. His mother, a godly woman, died when he was three, leaving his father to care for Blaise and his two sisters. The elder Pascal, Etienne, was a man of genuine devotion and ability, and he eagerly sought to stimulate the minds of his children. In order to improve their educational opportunities, he gave up his post as magistrate, and moved with his family to Paris in 1631.

The extraordinary gifts of the son began to appear very early. By the time he was twelve, having mastered Greek and Latin, his compulsive desire to find things out for himself led him to work through, on his own, the thirty-two geometric theorems of Euclid's *First Book*. When this almost unbelievable feat became known, he was invited to accompany his father to the weekly meetings of the Academy of Science, where he mingled freely with the greatest intellectuals of his day. Before he was sixteen, the young genius had unraveled the mystery of conic sections, composing a treatise which anticipated projective geometry. Thereafter, he discovered the famous lemma in mathematics which came to be called the Pascal theorem. Just as an aside, while still in his teens, he invented and constructed the first calculating machine, showing himself as skilled in applied science as in pure thought.

The Pascal household observed a nominal Catholic religious practice until 1646 when they came into contact with Jansenism. This group within the Roman Church, somewhat comparable to Protestant Puritans, stressed divine grace and election in redemption. Blaise embraced their teaching, and soon won over to his new faith the other members of his family. From this time on, he became a diligent student of the Bible and generally tried to follow a life of personal piety.

His resolution to "live only for God" did not keep him from continuing his scientific research. In the course of his experiments, he demonstrated the fact of atmospheric pressure, the vacuum, and the weight of air. These findings, published in 1647, led to his investigation of the equilibrium of liquids, establishing the principle of hydrodynamics. From these discoveries came the barometer, the vacuum pump, the air compressor, the syringe, and the hydraulic press. Not stopping with these practical applications of his thinking, he later explored the concept of universal, physical relativity and developed the theory of probability, from which emerged infinitesimal calculus. During this time, he advanced the axiom which was to become the guiding dictum of modern science—"that experiments are the true masters to follow in physics."

Interestingly, this passion for objective proof comes through in his treatment of theology, not in the sense that religious truth can be demonstrated through the human sciences or metaphysical reasoning, for it is of a supernatural order. But in its own order of knowledge, spiritual reality can be validated through the testimony of scripture, which Pascal believed to be "the Word of God infallible in the facts which it records." In this position, he came to reject the speculative approach of scholasticism and maintained that the Bible alone is our basis for the Christian faith. He recognized the importance of church councils and tradition in defining the proper interpretation, but insisted that no authoritative view can be contrary to the Bible. For, as he said, "He who will give the meaning of Scripture, and does not take it from Scripture, is an enemy of Scripture."

Pascal's father died in 1651, and soon afterward, his younger sister, Jacqueline, entered the Jansenist convent at Port-Royal (his older sister had married earlier). Bereft of family companionship, Blaise unwisely turned to some of his aristocratic friends to fill the void, and with them sought diversion in the pleasures of fashionable society. After a year or more of this attachment to the "world," he was left disillusioned and became more convinced than ever of the vanity of man. Neither the delight of idle amusement nor the renown of great achievement could satisfy his yearning soul. He was brought to the point of despair.

It was in this state that he was reading the scripture on that eventful evening in 1654 when God appeared to him in Fire. He had opened to the seventeenth chapter of John's Gospel where Jesus is seen in prayer before giving himself over to be crucified. As he read, suddenly the room was filled with the flaming Presence of him who is perfect holiness and love. The Word written in the Book was confirmed by the Word present in the Son. Here was certitude. Before such experiential Truth he could only bow in "total submission to Jesus Christ."

After this experience, called his "second conversion," the broken and penitent scholar saw even more clearly the futility of living for self. He renounced every resource of the fleshly nature and gave himself completely to the message of scripture. All his worldly endeavors were abandoned. He sold his coach and horses, his fine furniture and silverware, and gave the money to the poor. Even his extensive library was discarded, keeping only a few devotional books and his Bible. The glory of his Savior became his only concern. Never again would he ever sign his name to his own writings, nor let his name be mentioned in praise. Taking the guise of Monsieur de Mons, he left Paris, and went to live among the Jansenist "solitaries" of Port-Royal.

The views of this holiness sect were not popular in the more easy-going establishment of the Sorbonne and among the Jesuits. Eventually the pope was persuaded to condemn them. Amid the controversy, Pascal came forth to defend their cause. His vindication, appearing as *The Provincial Letters*, began in 1656 and established him as the most articulate polemist of his generation. The dialogues cast the whole dispute in simple logic, showing by withering irony and wit that the real issue was one of morality, not dogma. He did not deprecate official church doctrine, but decried the way clever maneuvering with words was being used to subvert the intent of scripture. Such casuistry he saw as a form of self-esteem, which therefore leads to concupiscence or creature love. To Pascal, the love of God alone motivates the body of Christ, and this love is evidenced by obedience to his word.

His *Letters* suddenly broke off in 1657, for his attention had focused on the larger task of constructing an *Apology for the Christian Religion*. It was designed to be a demonstration of Christianity, setting forth reasons which would convince the unbeliever. He planned to spend ten years on the work, but as it turned out, due to his early death there was time only to prepare his notes for the final draft. Ranging from a few cryptic words to short essays, the "thoughts" were collected by the Port-Royalists and published as the *Pensées* eight years after his death. The more than seven hundred fragments have come to be regarded as his greatest masterpiece.

Beginning with the human dilemma, he draws a picture of natural man's misery on the one hand and his glory on the other. There would be no meaning nor purpose in life apart from God's disclosure of his word. Indifference of the skeptic is overcome by means of a "wager," based on his law of probability, whereby everyone is confronted with an all-encompassing choice. God is or is not. One who responds in the affirmative has everything to gain and nothing to lose; whereas the person who denies God has nothing permanently to gain and everything to lose. Though it is self-interest which provokes the reasonable decision, still it causes one to move from a habit of disbelief and invites a new direction toward truth.

God's saving revelation, however, comes only through divine illumination in the believer's soul. "It is the heart which experiences God, and not the reason. This, then, is faith: God felt by the heart." By this Pascal does not mean mystical emotion, but rather, an intuitive love for God himself. Those awakened by grace will have this perception. Moreover, God has so constructed the universe that he will be found by those who search for him with all their heart.

The focus is Jesus Christ, the object of all scripture, for he alone incarnated the Infinite Word in our human estate. In his Person is revealed both the Truth of God and the truth of man. Yet only persons who renounce self-love will know what this means. Herein is exposed the error of those who do not find the Truth. A genuine Christian does not squabble over signs; he humbly bows in adoration before his majestic Lord.

A hurried reader, sitting in a cushioned rocker, with a box of chocolates at hand, probably will not derive much from the writings of Pascal. But the serious reader who pauses for reflection will be rewarded in mind and spirit. The following gems of thought, excerpted from the *Pensées*, signal the strata of riches to be discovered:

> *The Mystery of Jesus*—Jesus suffers in His passions the torments which men inflict upon Him, but in His agony He suffers the torments which He inflicts upon Himself. This is a suffering from no human, but an almighty hand, for He must be almighty to bear it.
>
> Jesus seeks some comfort at least in His three dearest friends, and they are asleep. He prays them to bear with Him for a little, and they leave Him with entire indifference, having so little compassion that it could not prevent their sleeping even for a moment. And thus Jesus was left alone to the wrath of God.
>
> Jesus is alone on the earth, without any one not only to feel and share His suffering, but even to know of it; He and Heaven were alone in that knowledge.
>
> Jesus is in a garden, not of delight as the first Adam, where he lost himself and the whole human race, but in one of agony, where He saved Himself and the whole human race.
>
> He suffers this affliction and this desertion in the horror of night.
>
> I believe that Jesus never complained but on this single

occasion; but then He complained as if he could no longer bear His extreme suffering. "My soul is sorrowful, even unto death."

Jesus seeks companionship and comfort from men. This is the sole occasion in all His life, as it seems to me. But He receives it not, for His disciples are asleep.

Jesus will be in agony even to the end of the world. We must not sleep during that time. (Article 552)

Do little things as though they were great, because of the majesty of Jesus Christ who does them in us, and who lives our life; and do the greatest things as though they were little and easy, because of His omnipotence. (Article 552)

It seems to me that Jesus Christ only allowed His wounds to be touched after His resurrection. We must unite ourselves only to His sufferings.

At the Last Supper He gave Himself in communion as about to die; to the disciples at Emmaus as risen from the dead; to the whole Church as ascended into Heaven. (Article 553)

Jesus Christ came to blind those who saw clearly, and to give sight to the blind; to heal the sick, and leave the healthy to die; to call to repentance, and to justify sinners, and to leave the righteous in their sins; to fill the needy, and leave the rich empty. (Article 770)

So I hold out my arms to my *Redeemer,* who, having been foretold for four thousand years, has come to suffer and to die for me on earth, at the time and under all the circumstances foretold. By His grace, I await death in peace, in the hope of being eternally united to Him. Yet I live with joy, whether in the prosperity which it pleases Him to bestow upon me, or in the adversity which He sends for my good, and which He has taught me to bear by His example. (Article 736)

He was still working on his *Pensées* when urged by some friends to solve a geometric problem which had baffled mathematicians for centuries. Thinking that it would give his Christian apology a greater hearing, and also to distract his mind from an incessant headache, he analyzed the nature of cycloid curves. His findings, published in 1658, laid the foundations for differential and integral calculus. In another moment of inventive genius, noticing the numbers of people walking long distances in Paris, he designed an omnibus carriage for public transport, which brought into being the world's first bus service. However, such scientific exploits were mere pastimes. His attention now was fixed on something far more profound. So engrossed was he in thought on spiritual things that he wrote in 1660, "I would not take two steps for geometry...I am engaged in studies so remote from such preoccupations that I can scarcely remember that they actually exist."

But the terrible pain which had punished him through most of his life grew worse, and finally he was unable to continue any mental exercise. One of the last things he wrote was "A Prayer Asking God to Use His Illness for a Good End." The following excerpt beautifully reflects his trust in the perfect will of God.

Lord, whose Spirit is so good and so gentle, and who is so compassionate that not only all prosperity but even all afflictions that come to thine elect are the results of Thy compassion...

Grant that I may conform to Thy will, just as I am, that, being sick as I am, I may glorify Thee in my sufferings. Without them I cannot attain to glory; without them, my Saviour, even Thou wouldst not have risen to glory. By the marks of Thy sufferings Thou dost recognize those who are Thy disciples. Therefore recognize me as Thy disciple by the ills that I endure, in my body and in my spirit, for the offenses which I have committed. And since nothing is pleasing to God unless it be offered to Him by Thee, unite my will with Thine and my sufferings with those that Thou hast suffered; grant that mine may become Thine. Unite me with Thee; fill me with Thee and Thy Holy Spirit. Enter into my heart and into my soul, there to bear my sufferings and to continue in me that part of the suffering of Thy passion which yet remains to be endured, whichThou art yet completing in Thy members until the perfect consummation of Thy Body, so that it shall no longer be I who live and suffer but that it shall be Thou who dost live and suffer in me, O my Saviour. And thus, having some small part in Thy suffering, I shall be filled wholly by Thee with the glory which it has brought to Thee, the glory in which Thou dost dwell with the Father and the Holy Spirit, forever and ever. Amen. (*Great Shorter Works of Pascal*, pp. 220-28)

On August 19, 1662, his intense bodily suffering ended. The awe-inspiring saint, with faith "simple as a child," died at the home of his brother-in-law, having turned his house over to an impoverished family. He was thirty-nine years old.

Few men have ever lived who thought more deeply upon the nature of reality. "At an age when others have hardly begun to see the light, he had completed the cycle of human knowledge," and seeing its emptiness, directed his remaining energies to know him in whom is hidden all the wisdom and the glory of God. Here Pascal found the answer to his heart's desire, and in that assurance, he discovered the Truth that sets men free—the Truth that every man can know by faith in Jesus Christ.

NINE

T. Stanley Soltau

by Charles Turner

S PRING, 1914. PRINCETON THEOLOGICAL SEMINARY. Two young
men are walking toward Miller Chapel. The taller—the red-
haired one—is Stanley Soltau, who will be graduating soon. His
companion is Arch Campbell, his future brother-in-law, a junior.
They are late for the Tuesday night meeting, but their pace is
unhurried as they round the stately privet hedge near the entrance.
The days are noticeably longer now, and it's as though the lingering
sunlight has beguiled them into thinking they have plenty of time.

Actually, the season has little to do with it except in a
cumulative way. Neither student has missed a Tuesday night
meeting since the beginning of the academic year, and Stanley is
wondering what harm it would do if they were to sit this one out.

Before they reach the steps, he slows to a halt. He turns to the
other and says, "What say, Arch, let's skip the meeting tonight and
go to my room and talk."

"It's all right by me," Arch replies.

Stanley gives the matter a second thought. He knows that he
should set a good example for the younger student. Besides, it

would be a shame to mar their record at this point. He says, "Perhaps we ought to go on, after all, but let's sit in the back row so we can skip out if we like."

The Tuesday night meetings are, as the Princeton Seminary Bulletin states, "for devotion and for instruction in general lines of Christian activity." These assemblies are in addition to the regular evening prayers, which every student is expected to attend. Because this is the first Tuesday in the month, the program will be under the direction of professors rather than students, and there will be a speaker on missions and a "concert of prayer" for missions around the world.

Although Stanley's interest on this occasion is less than stalwart, he is not indifferent to the subject of missions. He was born into a missionary family and for most of his life he has believed that God will give him the same vocation. Indeed, it is for this kind of endeavor that he has been preparing himself during these years at seminary. A mission field is out there waiting for him—of that he feels certain. Which mission field? Well, Stanley is curious about the geography of his future, but he has stopped sniffing around in every direction trying to precede the Lord. He is confident that he will know the appointed region at the right time. If there is a question that nags him about any aspect of missionary life ahead, it is this: is it fair to ask Molly, his fiancée, to abandon her family and all the familiar furnishings of her culture to follow him into a strange realm where circumstances are uncertain and the outlook promises one strenuous adjustment after another? This, it occurs to him as he and her brother enter the chapel, is what he subconsciously has been wanting to talk about.

The meeting has begun. The crowd is thicker than usual. With everyone standing for the hymn, it is difficult to tell exactly where the empty seats are. The back row is full, they discover, and so is the next row. By the time they find two seats near the aisle, they are deep in the tide of male voices and closer to the front than they are to the doors. Professor B.B. Warfield, who is to introduce the speaker, sends a nod, almost a smile, to absolve their tardiness.

Stanley realizes that he and Arch are speared to the pew. There will be no vanishing act tonight.

What he does not realize—not at first—is that the perspectives of his life are lined up and he now has moved into a position where, captive, he will see his past and his future come together with precision, to a focus that will define each more distinctly than ever before.

The speaker is Dr. George Shannon McCune.

The mission of concern is Korea, where Dr. McCune is head-master of a Christian academy.

At least two listeners *hear,* and one of them is Stanley Soltau.

He was to look back on that evening as an example of man's footsteps and determinations being swallowed up in the mystery of God's sovereignty, for it was then and there that "the land of the morning calm" reached out and claimed him.

In those days, thirty-five years before the resounding Korean conflict of the mid-century, that country was little known in the Western world except as Japan's booty from the Russo-Japanese War of 1904-5. Stanley Soltau knew its location on the globe, could put his finger to it, even knew of the Presbyterian mission there, and yet he usually thought of Korea in vague and subtractive terms: it was neither China nor Japan, it somehow was "neither this nor that." Certainly, before that evening, he had never felt a pull in its direction. Perhaps that was because it was an established field and he had longed for the challenge and romance of uncharted territory. But on the other hand, perhaps it was due to the fact that Korea, as a ministry, had not received the wide journalistic coverage that some countries had, and he simply had overlooked its invitation. Whatever the reason for his delayed interest, it was of the past and did not lessen his enthusiasm for the call. His recognition of divine guidance was so strong that he knew, even before Molly responded to his letter about it, that she would perceive it too, and that she would be at his side when he journeyed to the Orient. His reservations about subjecting her to hardships lost out to his acknowledged need of a helpmeet and his vision of her as the best missionary wife ever.

Stanley Soltau was born in 1890, on the island of Tasmania, forty minutes after the arrival of his brother, David Livingston Soltau. Their parents, who had not suspected that twins were in store, had hoped for a boy and already had chosen the name of the famous missionary-explorer. When the surprising gift of the second boy (their eighth child and sixth son) was delivered, they named him Theodore Stanley—Theodore for its meaning ("gift of God") and, appropriately enough, Stanley for the newspaper correspondent who followed Livingston to Africa. David was called David, but Theodore was known by his middle name throughout his life.

Another historic name linked with the Soltau twins is that of J. Hudson Taylor, founder of the China Inland Mission, who, on a visit to Tasmania when they were small, laid his hands upon them in a dedication service. His life intersected theirs again when they were ten years old and living in England, on which occasion he offered his hands once again, this time in a firm and memorable clasp as he inquired about their Christian growth and bequeathed to them as much of himself as he could.

The Soltau family came from a Plymouth Brethren tradition. The twins' paternal grandfather, Henry William Soltau, born in Plymouth in 1805, gave up his law practice to devote himself to the study of scripture. Both his scholarship and his spirituality are reflected in his writings, which are considered classics and are in print today: *The Holy Vessels and Furniture of the Tabernacle* and *The Tabernacle, the Priesthood and the Offerings* (Kregel Publications). Adding to that heritage was the visible ministry and example of their parents, George and Grace. It would seem merely a thematic progression that the Soltau twins, each in his own time, each in his own calling, became servants of the Word.

After accompanying their parents to the United States on a speaking tour in 1904, they stayed on and received schooling at Morningside Academy in Sioux City and at Northwestern University. Summers and long holidays were spent in Seattle, their family's "headquarters" in the States. Not the least of the attractions in that city of hills overlooking Puget Sound was a girl named Mary Campbell. David and Stanley became close friends of her brothers and were welcomed on a regular basis into the Presbyterian household of her parents. The hospitality of Joseph and Anna Campbell was so unfeigned and easygoing that they had sanctioned a veritable dorm in the upper reaches of their weathered gray manor on 88th Street.

Mary—who was to be Molly in Stanley's life—was brown-haired and hazel-eyed, as statuesque as a Gibson Girl, with the clean planes of bone structure that cinematographers look for. She was, in the flesh, the fair and winsome heroine of the romantic novels of the era. Her own love story began one day when, in the flurry of a girlish emotion, she sailed into the arms of the nearest male, whom she took to be her brother. The house being rampant with males, and the blur of her tears having misdirected her, she found herself in the appreciative embrace of Stanley. In years to come, when her daughters were old enough to delight in hearing of it, she would relate the incident many times, never remembering exactly what had caused the tears, but always remembering the warmth and the special stillness she had drawn from her comforter.

Stanley was rather shy with girls, according to his own reports, and he feared that Mary's eyes were only for his twin: David was an extravert and a charmer. But her pleasant mistake emboldened Stanley to court her outright. And her seemingly chance gravitation toward the shy one was prophetic. It was to him that her heart turned later, sure of its compass and with promises to last a lifetime.

As the younger twin prevailed in that situation, so must he prevail in this narrative. David Soltau's life was interesting in its own right (he went to Korea too, taught physics there, and after returning to the States, became an Episcopal priest and taught physics at Redlands University), but his story is for someone else to tell. David Soltau I did not know. Stanley Soltau I knew and respected and liked. He was my pastor in his later years. He himself was the inspiration for this portrait I'm attempting, and he himself was the basic source of my research.

I advanced many questions in the hope of gathering material for a full biography. He had kept no journals, no copies of his correspondence, and even though his memory was a large and colorful canvas, I was not able to extract from its richness the kind of order and detail necessary for the comprehensive treatment I had in mind. But I did glean enough to encourage me to put him on paper in one shorter form or another, someday. Now is someday, and it has occurred to me that perhaps I can capture Stanley Soltau's likeness and tell of his life faithfully in a sequence of brief glimpses, compressing his years for their essence, while I might have lost him—or, worse, misrepresented him—in a longer work.

Through the influence of the Campbell family, Stanley adopted a Presbyterian view of scripture, especially in regard to its emphasis on God's covenant promises. Perhaps his personality also played a part in the shift, his natural reserve tending toward a more precise approach to worship than the one in which he had grown up. A result of this development was his choice of Princeton Theological Seminary for further education. He financed his tuition himself by summer work as a surveyor in the state of Washington.

After graduation in May 1914, he was ordained to the ministry and commissioned by the Board of Foreign Missions of the Presbyterian Church in the U.S.A. He and Molly married in August, and in October they set out on the long voyage toward their first Korean winter. On the horizon, knowable even before the days were fulfilled, was the bleakness of Christmas in a strange land. Stanley was surprised to find that he suffered as keenly as Molly the loss of all that was familiar. Despite a warm welcome from fellow missionaries and Korean Christians, the loneliness for family and friends was like a tunnel through which they had to pass, and in which they had to reaffirm their belief that God truly had called them to this remote post.

The sense of strangeness, common to aliens in every culture, persisted after the doubts had lifted. It was intensified of course by the realization that *they*, Stanley and Molly, were the curiosities. Westerners seldom were seen in rural districts, and often the couple found that paper doors and windows had been perforated neatly by wet fingers for the convenience of inquisitive eyes. Sometimes the discovery was immediate: they would think they were enjoying the privacy of a closed shelter, and then, hearing themselves discussed in detail just beyond the thin barrier, they would know they were being observed with amusement.

Even more disconcerting was the laughter which surfaced from time to time when he was preaching. An early incident involved a boy who broke into snickering when Stanley happened to glance at him in the middle of a sermon. Stanley supposed that an incorrect verb ending had prompted the glee. His next glance brought forth the same effect. I am making one blunder after another, he thought. He concluded the sermon quickly and went on to the thoroughly practiced grammar of the Lord's Supper. But his language teacher was present and informed him that mistakes had been fewer than usual, that the eruptions had been caused by matters more difficult to remedy. The teacher was Korean and two years his junior, and it was an awkward moment as Oriental courtesy gave way to brotherly candor. "You see, Pastor, you are too tall and your hair is such a strange color and your nose is so big and your eyes are so deeply set in your head. This boy is a country boy, not used to seeing foreigners. He could not keep from laughing."

Bouts of homesickness prepared Stanley for counseling prospective missionaries later on. They would feel disconnected at times, he would warn them. They would, in a small measure, enter into the loneliness of Christ, whose ministry on earth he saw as the basic foreign mission experience. It was always a case of having been amputated from one's natural environment. "But," he would tell them, "it is in this loneliness that the companionship of the Lord becomes a blessed reality."

He spent three years in Syenchun, in the north, a railroad town of mud-walled houses thatched with rice straw. Nestled against hills known as the Dragon's Back, and entrenched in ancient superstition deeply enough to claim the dragon as the town guardian,

Syenchun was nonetheless a Christian center boasting two churches, two academies (one for girls, one for boys) and a well-staffed hospital. Stanley's main assignment there was language study, but his duties included teaching English and Bible to some of the classes in the boys' academy. He enjoyed playing tennis with the boys, and since none of them spoke English, the activity with them helped him to learn their language and to get to know them.

Among the students was pleasant-faced Chinsoo Kim, who was working his way through school. Chinsoo's parents, like many other poor Korean farmers, had moved into Manchuria to escape the increasingly severe Japanese taxation. When he learned that the Soltaus would be taking the gospel to the settlements in Manchuria, he felt that he had something in common with them—an interest above the border. His father and mother, both Christians, had placed great importance upon his attending the academy. Only for the sake of his Christian education had he remained in Syenchun. Now that he was separated from them, he turned to Stanley and Molly for the warmth of a family, visiting often in their home, bringing his problems there, seeking advice about his future. He was quite serious about his own faith in Christ, and they grew to love him like a son.

In the years to come, Chinsoo would attend college and seminary and be ordained as a minister himself. During those years of further study, he would continue to visit in their home at every opportunity, wherever that home happened to be. (After Syenchun, they were stationed for a while in other towns in the north, and then for seventeen years in Chungju, in the south.) The Soltau children, as they came along, regarded Chinsoo as an elder brother who was always good for play. He manifested his devotion to the family by leading their newly purchased milk cow the three hundred miles to Chungju when they moved. Later, when he was pastor of the third congregation in Syenchun, he and Stanley would see each other at meetings of the General Assembly. Stanley could count on Chinsoo to be absolutely honest with him when there was friction between the Korean pastors and some of the missionaries. Their "father and son" relationship allowed a communication which helped to solve problems when the Korean pastors rightly insisted that they were grown and could think for themselves.

The mission had been in Korea almost thirty years when Stanley arrived. Its policy from the beginning had been to establish national churches that were self-supporting, self-governing, and self-propagating. In this the pioneers had followed the example of Dr. J.L. Nevious, a Presbyterian missionary in Shantung, China. Most mission boards in that day considered the practice a radical innovation, but Stanley embraced the principle as his personal philosophy of mission, seeing it as apostolic in heritage and therefore the most workable and promising method of planting the gospel in every land. His own observations proved to him that it was the one way to ensure natural, sturdy church growth. It was the opposite of colonialism. The dignity of the nationals remained intact, for essential in the process was a point beyond which the "foreign" missionaries could not lord it over them as benefactors and decision-makers.

While the Soltaus were stationed in the north, Stanley made numerous journeys into Manchuria. These mission projects required that he be separated from Molly and the little ones for weeks at a stretch. Molly's brother Arch, who had accompanied Stanley to that Tuesday night meeting at Princeton Seminary, was now serving under the same mission. He and his family were also stationed in the north, so Molly did not feel quite so alone when Stanley was away. The two families lived together for a while in a house in Kangkai. They called the house Camelot. The Arthurian connotation seemed to fit the mood of the residence, and it was a wonderful place for little cousins to romp.

Often the travel in Manchuria was crude and sluggish. Stanley tackled the mountainous distances by various means—pony, bicycle, sled, raft, dugout, bean boat—and he covered many a mile on foot. Against typhoid, and against the diminutive fish swimming in the pots of cool drinking water at the inns, he was armed with chlorine. Against the powers of darkness, he was armed with the Word. The name of Jesus, so far as Stanley knew, had never been spoken in many of the villages he entered. It was an awesome experience to approach a community like that and think about his privilege and his responsibility. It was also extremely humbling. In those moments he felt an acute kinship with missionaries Paul and Patrick and Brainerd and Livingston and Taylor, and with all of those messengers who before him had announced the gospel in localities where it had never been heard. One of his goals was to help establish churches among the expatriate Korean Christians, but he was always conscious of his duty to evangelize, and he saw the life of Christ take hold and grow in areas where there had been no former witness.

Frequent absences from home continued as a way of life after his move to Chungju. He was in charge of a circuit of churches in the province and had to visit all of them regularly. His itinerary took him through rice fields and pine forests and valleys showered with persimmons and walnuts. The persimmons were giant, dusted with natural sugar after the first frost, and the walnuts were a white variety, paper-shelled and delicious. On homeward jaunts, in season, Stanley would lade himself with selections for the family larder. By the fifth year in Chungju, there were four children: Eleanor, Mary, George, and Addison. The girls were born in the north, the boys in the south. (A third daughter, Theodora, born during a furlough in Seattle, had died of diphtheria at the age of two.) Molly never had to wonder what to do with her time when Stanley was away. In addition to the usual business of motherhood, she undertook the schooling of her brood, and, with the professional guidance of Calvert correspondence courses, saw each of them through the sixth grade at home.

The year 1936 brought difficult times for the Korean church. The Japanese government, attempting to unify the empire in preparation for the war it was planning, decreed that students and faculty of every school in the domain must attend ceremonies at the State Shinto shrines. It was not simply a matter of being present and accounted for: obeisance was to be done before the sun goddess, Amaterasu-Omi-Kami, patron saint of the Japanese army and mythical ancestress of the imperial household. A profound bow was required of all. Mission schools were not exempt—they were in fact a major target. The church was the one institution over which the Japanese had not been able to gain control, and for that reason it was continually an object of suspicion. Shrines were erected near every school, and one by one they sprang up in every village of any size throughout the land. The day was foreseen—and it did come—when all churches and the entire population of Korea were included in the order.

Although the main purpose behind the order might have been to inculcate a spirit of patriotism among the Koreans, who were regarded as Japanese subjects, the move did violence to the religious freedom promised in the constitution. It did especial violence to the hearts of those individuals whose God had said, "Thou shalt have no other gods. . . . Thou shalt not bow down to them." Many Christians were loyal to that first commandment and resolved to suffer persecution rather than comply with the ruling. Others wondered if perhaps they should consider attendance at the shrines a civic duty and the compulsory bow merely a patriotic gesture.

Stanley, as Chairman of the Executive Committee of the Mission, stood against compromise. After his meetings with high officials in the government availed no leniency for Christians, he took the position that it would be better to close the mission schools than to go along with Shinto worship. Worship was what it was, he believed. The separation of State Shinto from Sectarian Shinto had been effected for the appearance of insuring religious freedom, but it actually had cleared the way for forced participation in the State Shinto ceremonies, which now were promoted as nonreligious even though prayers and oblations were essential. The misrepresentations confused very few people who took their Christianity—or their Buddhism, or their Shinto—seriously. Dr. Kato Genchi, of the Imperial University of Tokyo, had stated in his 1935 treatise on Shinto, "I regard National Shinto, embracing both Kokutai Shinto and Jinja Shinto, as a variety of religion—a religion with aspects differing from those of Buddhism and Christianity, but nevertheless always a religion."

Most of the missionaries supported Stanley and voted to close the schools if demands were pressed. This was not an easy policy to adopt. Every session of the mission and every committee meeting was haunted by a member of the police who was present to kill discussion of the shrines. The government, next to its insistence on school participation, was determined that those schools not close, for such action would place a burden on its own education system.

Demands *were* pressed.

A number of schools *did* close.

Persecution began.

The mission board back in the United States approved the mission's decision at first, but later, treating the question primarily as an administrative matter, resorted to a formal silence on the basic issue of idolatry. Among their concerns was the fact that mission properties were at stake. The silence served to uphold the minority who believed that the schools should remain open at any price. Stanley saw the board's attitude, in principle, as a bow toward Amaterasu-Omi-Kami.

The arguments for acquiescence seemed to boil down to these points: God knew the circumstances, knew the hearts of the students and faculty, knew the difference between an act of patriotism and an act of reverence. Surely a token bow to a nonexistent deity in a toylike shrine would not offend the true and reasonable God. Would it not be preferable to snuffing out the means of Christian education which had operated so successfully in the past? The bending would be physical, not spiritual.

Stanley had never thought of himself as holding a full-fledged sacramental view, but he realized that at this juncture he could not divorce that which was physical and visible from that which was spiritual and invisible.

"Not so much as a nod of the head should be offered," he said at the beginning of the troubles, and he never slackened his advice. In his opinion it was no more possible to associate the worship of the sun goddess with the worship of Jesus Christ than it was in the days of Elijah to associate the worship of Baal with the worship of Jehovah.

Within a few years, according to figures released by the police, sixty thousand Korean Christians were arrested and thrown into jail.

In the summer of 1937, in the thick of the controversy and before the tyranny had reached its peak, the Soltaus' furlough came due. The girls were in college in the United States, having finished their high school education at a boarding academy in Pyeng Yang. Stanley and Molly and the boys, traveling north toward Vladivostok, where they would board the Trans-Siberian Express to journey home by way of England, passed through Syenchun, Stanley's first post, the town where Chinsoo Kim was now pastor of a new and growing church. Stanley had sent word to Chinsoo. He knew that the young man would be at the train station to say good-bye. He looked forward to seeing him and wished that they could have a long talk instead of the brief chat the scheduled stop would permit. The shadows under which they were living caused a man to treasure his friendships.

As the train approached the Dragon's Back and the thatched roofs of Syenchun began to multiply, Stanley gave himself to thoughts of those earlier days. It seemed natural at this point to summarize the years since then. It was not so much a matter of taking stock as it was of letting his memories and his previous summations come upon him freely.

One hut in particular caught his attention. It reminded him of the hut to which he had been called on his first itinerating trip. His main duties—the duties for which he had been prepared—were preaching and administering the sacraments of baptism and the Lord's Supper. But when he arrived at the last church on the circuit, he was asked to visit a demon-possessed woman. With trepidation he had followed the concerned Christians who led the way. They explained to him that the woman had watched an exorcist driving evil spirits out of another house, and that while she was standing there, a demon had taken residence in her! Stanley entered the hut and found a shambles. The woman lay on the floor, a revolting sight, muttering unintelligibly. The husband and three small boys stood by helpless. She was bound hand and foot to restrain her from tearing off her clothes and doing further damage to the dwelling. Stanley read portions of scripture. She would quiet only when he spoke the name of Jesus. After prayer, he commanded the demon to come out of her. He had never received ecclesiastical instruction in the procedure, but he did the best he could.

He suggested that she be brought to the mission hospital in Syenchun if there was no improvement. This was done. But little was accomplished except for the benefits of soap and water and the forcing of nourishment. After her release from the hospital, he arranged for a Bible woman to take her in for a while. Other Bible women were asked to come and pray over her. Stanley had a profound respect for the work of those mature women disciplined in scripture and prayer. Confrontation with demons was almost a specialty with them, so often had they seen deliverance. This time the women applied themselves for weeks in an unceasing circle of attendance and supplication, and they all agreed that it was a very stubborn case. Their prayers were finally answered when the woman was taken to church at their insistence. "Where am I?" she had asked during the service, and from then on she was normal. The demon had left silently, without the usual climactic display, its violence defeated at last by the gift of peace. Stanley remembered that the woman and all of her family became believers in Jesus Christ.

It occurred to him that she might have become a Bible woman herself in the years he had been gone from that circuit. It was impossible for him to keep up with every convert on an individual basis. The Korean church was too large for that. One thing was sure: there had been opportunity for her to become a Bible *student*, at least. The reason for the rapid growth of the Korean church, he felt, was the importance placed on Bible study. With week-long Bible conferences held in every district once a year, and with attendance seldom dropping below the total baptized membership, Korean Christians as a whole could be called "Bible people." Although Stanley was pleased to have had a part in that emphasis, he realized that a strong factor in the success of the conferences was the average Korean's studious temperament and desire for knowledge. He knew Korean farmers who walked for more than two hundred miles round-trip to attend the conferences, their daily rice on their backs.

But all the lay scholars and Bible women and delivered personalities receded when he thought about Chinsoo Kim. In Stanley's personal mosaic of Korean Christianity, Chinsoo was always there, prominent, an excellent image to represent all of the national pastors. The fact that he was like family was beside the point, Stanley tried to tell himself. Yet he knew that "a father's heart" was involved.

The train lurched to stillness.

There Chinsoo was now, outside the window, waiting on the platform as Stanley had known he would be. Nearby stood three other Korean pastors of the area, and in a separate cluster stood their wives. Chinsoo had moved out from under the roof and was shielding his eyes. His white cotton took the sun cleanly, telling of a woman's care. He had married, but Stanley and Molly had never met his wife. Stanley matched the other pastors with their wives, and he was disappointed to find that Chinsoo's had not come to the station.

George and Addison, aged thirteen and eleven, disembarked on their own and made straight for Chinsoo. He boxed them warmly, then directed his attention to Stanley and Molly as they stepped down from the train. He placed his hands before him in the attitude of ceremonial courtesy. He bent slightly.

Stanley's right hand went to Chinsoo's shoulder, not disrespectful of the formality but ending it nevertheless. After an exchange of greetings with Chinsoo, Molly turned toward the women who waited for their visit. Stanley talked with the other pastors for a minute or so. Chinsoo, at the first opportunity, pulled him aside for a few words in private. They walked along the platform.

"How is your wife?" Stanley asked. "I'm sorry she didn't come with you."

"She is well. She honors us with her absence, knowing my desire to speak alone with you as long as possible. She is a person small of body, but she has a very large mind."

"Does she make good squash soup?" It seemed to Stanley that good squash soup could accomplish in Syenchun the same wonders that a winning cherry pie could accomplish in Seattle.

Chinsoo said, "Yes—and she makes good kimchee."

Stanley said, "I am relieved to hear that!"

They laughed. The turnip pickle dear to the Korean palate was dear to Stanley's palate too. His love of kimchee was almost a matter of pride with him. It was a food that most missionaries had learned to swallow but not to enjoy.

Time was short. Chinsoo grew serious as they started back. "Father, I fear that hard times are ahead for us in this country. We cannot tell what will happen. We cannot tell what we shall be called upon to face. I shall miss your leadership while you are gone, but your past counsel will sustain us."

"It is the Lord who will sustain you."

"It is you who have spoken his word to me. Pray that I shall be strong in that word when the time comes."

"I shall indeed."

"The stand we are taking against shrine worship—tell me again that we are doing the right thing. Some people are likely to suffer dire consequences. It must not be for less than the honor of Christ. This *is* the issue, is it not?"

Stanley gave it thought once more. He wished he could say something that would alleviate the situation and prevent further suffering. Still, he knew that a weaker position would never be acceptable to Chinsoo or to himself.

"There is no question about it," he said.

The train shook. Departure was imminent. Chinsoo took from

his pocket a folded piece of paper and pressed it into Stanley's hand. A chorus of good-byes lifted, but Chinsoo's was the voice that lingered in the ear as Stanley followed Molly and the boys into the car.

When the waving was over and the assemblage at the station had dispersed, one figure remained. Chinsoo was visible until the station itself was lost behind a curve.

Stanley settled against the ungiving seat. He opened the paper. *My dear Father,* the note began, *May the peace of God accompany you and Mother and the boys on your long journey and take you to your home in safety. As for us, I fear that hard days are ahead . . .* Here was repeated most of what Chinsoo had spoken in person. Evidently he had written the thoughts down in case he did not find a chance to express them face to face, yet the tone of the note was stronger, more positive . . . *Of one thing I am certain, you will never feel ashamed of your son. Whatever comes, I am looking to the Lord for his enabling power, so that in all things I shall be faithful to him and shall never deny him or bring disgrace to his name. Your loving son, Chinsoo.*

The Soltaus were unable to return to Korea. Toward the end of their furlough, Stanley was felled by intense pain that turned out to be a large kidney stone. Surgery was required. By the time he had recuperated, the mission horizon was darkening with World War II. The terminology "postponement of plans" had to be dropped, finally, for the more realistic "cancellation of plans." (Arch Campbell and his wife, still in Korea when the Japanese attacked Pearl Harbor, remained on duty for the duration of the war. Stanley's brother David had left Korea years earlier.) Unwelcome though the situation was, the closing of the door simplified the step that soon was necessary for Stanley—necessary if he was to live up to his conscience. His strong convictions against the mission board's continuing laxity of principle regarding Shinto shrine worship led him into ministry outside the denomination.

From 1942 until 1968 he was pastor of First Evangelical Church in Memphis, Tennessee. The congregation was, and is, a mix of believers from various denominations, a flock desirous of biblical preaching. Founded in 1935, the church was in many ways typical of the independent drift which marked that decade and has widened since. And yet, while severed from historic liturgy, Stanley Soltau with his inborn dignity kept the services from wandering off into too surprising informality, the brambles of which seemed to snag and impair any sense of worship in some of the breakaway "fundamental" Bible churches. His stress on the preaching of the Word was balanced by his concern that the service preceding the sermon be objective preparation and not subjective entertainment. His view of Christ as friend and mediator did not lower his view of Christ as the Majestic and Holy One. He did not approach the wonders of Word and sacrament in a casual or cheeky manner. I was a member of that church during his years there, and to me it was as though Stanley Soltau, like the prophet Isaiah, had seen the Lord "high and lifted up."

On Sundays from October to June he appeared in morning dress, evoking the formalities of an era gone, a civilization swept from the earth by two world wars and the inflow of windy new ideas about what was important and what was not. From that previous civilization—let's say, from the world of Princeton Theological Seminary, 1912-14—he had let nothing slide that he could hold stationary. He had held to worthwhile custom as tenaciously as he had held to sound Christian doctrine, although he never would have confused their imports. To those individuals who remembered the vanished proprieties, the figure he cut was nostalgic, no doubt. To those of us who were younger, of a more slipshod generation, he appeared merely *interesting*—and something of a show, which was the last thing he would have wished. But I would take nothing for that show as I screen it in my memory, and I thank him for it. I see the tails of his black cutaway lifting in the November gust as he rounds the back of his Oldsmobile to open the door for his wife. Beneath his homburg he is mostly bald now, but a glint of red is visible in the cropped gray remainder near his ears. I see Molly, coiffed and hatted, come forth serenely at his arm to be spirited up the church steps. Even that brief "film clip" somehow reminds me that *every* Sunday is Easter, and that a meeting with the Risen One is an affair to perk up about.

He spoke an English that was very close to the king's. He said he had learned to speak several languages, but "southern" wasn't one of them. It was true. After twenty-five years in Memphis, his a's, while not as broad as they once had been, held their own to the degree that they still had to be dealt with by the southern ear. Perhaps this added, not fairly, to the unease with which some people viewed him as an authority figure. He *was* an authority figure, and I believe that such an image is the fleshing out of a scriptural principle. I found that some people disliked Stanley Soltau for the very reasons that I liked him. In this day of clamorous individualism, which has touched churches as well as every area of our culture, I still like an authority figure—one who doesn't abuse the image, of course. I still want to hear a servant of the Word say, "Thus saith the Lord," and not "My idea is this, what's yours?"

He preached from the Old Testament often, and deeply, but even there his themes were so Christocentric that the gospel grew richer and richer. His sermons were too long by today's standards and I agree that most of them could have been improved by a tightening of five or ten minutes, but ears that listened all the way received immeasurable content, all of it applicable in a life of faith. His pastoral prayers were lengthy too, never less than ten minutes, but those individuals who stayed awake were carried to the throne of God with confession and praise and an orderly raising of supplications, the list of which encompassed the world. A major theme of his preaching was *Possessing the possessions that are yours in Christ*—and he wasn't talking about Cadillacs and swimming pools. Another recurring theme was *God's presence with his covenant people.* I thank him for unfolding this truth, which for me contains a wealth of New Testament realities, especially when viewed in connection with the Eucharist.

Doctor Soltau, he was called. I sometimes called him Pastor Soltau, or simply Pastor, for I like the meaning *and* the sound of that word, but usually for everyone it was "Doctor Soltau." He was known—and known by that handle—in evangelical circles well beyond the Memphis area. He identified with the conservative Presbyterian movement and, while still with the independent church in Memphis, joined the denomination which became Reformed Presbyterian Church, Evangelical Synod (which, ten years after his death, would lose its name in union with the Presbyterian Church in America). From 1958 until 1972 he was President of World Presbyterian Missions. Other boards on which he served were North Africa Mission, Greater Europe Mission, and Covenant Theological Seminary. He imparted to his congregation a concern for missionary work, and under his ministry the church designated 51 percent of its income to missions. After his retirement from pastoral duties, he renewed his own foreign missionary endeavor by making himself available to various boards. He traveled extensively for three years, on this or that assignment. He had lived to see the jet age and he was very much a part of it. He was "on the go" at eighty, for missions were still on his mind.

The freedom to pack up and leave and trace the curve of the earth again and again was not without its sadness. His Molly, whose regal posture had been destroyed over the years by rheumatoid arthritis, whose hands had frozen into an awkwardness that expressed the pain in which she was imprisoned, died in an automobile accident in 1969. Until his retirement, she had kept up certain appearances and made it a point to stand at his side at the church door after every sermon, but during the next year—her last—she became totally crippled and was dependent on him to assist her every move. He cared for her hour by hour. Had she not been taken from him, he would have been unavailable elsewhere. But he knew that her release was far more blessed than his. He was driving when the accident occurred, and although not at fault, he at first was tormented by the thought that he should have been more cautious at the intersection. On the other hand, when the young man who ran the stop light visited the Soltau house on the day after the death, begging forgiveness, he was met by a Stanley Soltau who was able to console him and pray for him and openly thank God for the fact that Mary Soltau, his own dear Molly, would suffer no more.

He told me that on one of his trips, on a jet to Brazil, he happened to be seated next to a girl of ten or eleven, of Spanish descent and obviously from a Roman Catholic background, who spoke delightful English. Being the Protestant Evangelical missionary that he was, he asked her, after they had chatted for a while, if she knew Jesus Christ as her Lord and Savior. He said that she looked up at him with steady eyes and said, "Indeed I do. I pray to him every day to make me a better servant of his." With that, he said, they settled back and enjoyed fellowship the rest of the flight. This man who would make an issue when the issue involved loyalty to Christ was happy to overlook differences on a personal level if basic Christian oneness was evident. His dividing line and his grounds of communion were clear. He would not have thought of himself as an ecumenist, and surely he wasn't in a loose or compromising way, but perhaps he was an example of the ideal one. His denominator was not low. It was always as high as the position to which Christ had ascended.

Serious as he was about foreign missions, he never made the person who was not a foreign missionary feel that he or she was involved in the lesser glory of God. He was truly gracious to me in this respect. A writer of fiction, in the estimation of some Christians, is not exactly "about his father's business." But Stanley Soltau read my stories and seemed to enjoy them. Now and then he would ask me, "What are you working on?" and I would say something like "Oh, a little trash." His comment would be on this order: "Good trash, I hope." He told me that as he browsed in airport newsstands in search of reading material to pass the miles away he seldom saw anything "fit to read" or that he would wish to "be seen with." He believed there was a definite need for good short stories and novels, and his sanction was a freeing influence in my own work.

His interest in "the indigenous church" as a mission ideal had not waned when his work in Korea ended. He had continued to support the concept at every opportunity. His book on the subject, *Missions at the Crossroads* (Van Kampen Press, 1954), found a receptive readership and its wake spilled over denominational boundaries, contributing to the swell of changing views that would have an impact on post-World War II missions. He was firm in his statement that Christian outreach would never be at the crossroads in regard to message (the gospel would always be "the power of God unto salvation to everyone that believeth"), but he felt that history was pressing down, that it was necessary for boards in general to determine and adopt the best method of completing the task of world evangelization.

I began to comprehend the book's influence one afternoon in 1970 as I talked with Pastor Paul Martens in his study at Trinity Lutheran Church in downtown Memphis. *Missions at the Crossroads* stood shoulder to shoulder with other mission books on a crowded shelf behind his desk. Martens had served from 1939 until 1949 as a missionary in China, and was in his fourteenth year on the mission board of Lutheran Church-Missouri Synod. He told me that Soltau, not long after the book's publication, had been invited to lecture at Concordia Seminary in St. Louis, where his missions perspective had gained esteem. Martens, who had heard him there, said that his appreciation of Soltau's viewpoint was grounded in his own experience in China. "We had been moving along the same lines," he said, "and I fully agreed with his conclusions." Because Martens had been forced out of China by Communist oppression, he saw that a major advantage of autonomous national churches was the fact that, no matter what political surge might evict the foreign missionary, a Christian constituency would remain in the land, active cells in the body of Christ. Those churches which had been allowed to mature on their own would survive and grow, even if underground.

Soltau's post-retirement responsibilities directed him to various corners of the earth, but not back to Korea. He returned there only once—in 1952, while the Communist conflict was still raging. It was not a journey into the past, for the past was no longer there, a new oppression having replaced the former one. But it was good to renew old friendships and learn of Christ's presence in the continuing tumult.

He had not heard from Chinsoo Kim since the day they talked at the station in Syenchun. Now he learned what had transpired. A few weeks after they had said good-bye, Chinsoo was arrested by the Japanese police because of his refusal to do obeisance to the sun goddess. He was sent to Pyongyong and imprisoned there with many other Christians. After a year or two, his wife was permitted to visit him, but he had been tortured so effectively that he failed to recognize her. She never saw him again. A friend of his, passing the jail one winter day, saw a pile of corpses, frozen, stacked like cordwood. He perused them and his gaze fell upon the icy husk of Chinsoo.

I believe that Soltau, from the moment he heard of Chinsoo's sacrifice, carried that death around with him just as he carried the death of Christ around with him. He understood that Chinsoo's death was a part of that greater and salutary death. The one obedience was in union with the other obedience. Chinsoo was Soltau's closest "family connection" to have been called to enter bodily into the drama of redemption and the fellowship of Christ's sufferings. Soltau did not speak of Chinsoo often. When he did tell the story, it was clear that he was not able to tell it as matter-of-factly as he would have liked.

His own death was gentle and quiet, in 1972, only three months after the death of his twin brother. There was no warning. He was at home in Memphis, in his comfortable chair at the end of a summer day. His hands passed from stillness to stillness without dropping the book he was reading.

Were he alive today as I write this, I think I might ask him, "Does it ever burden you that Chinsoo Kim and many other Korean Christians gave up their lives following your counsel when you yourself were freed from the dire situation and from experiencing or even viewing the consequences of your endorsed stand?" No disrespect would edge the question. I would be going for character, sure of the character to be revealed.

I of course do not know what he would answer—what he *would have answered*. I suspect, though, he would have offered a simple and undertoned "yes" and then gone on to explain that the burden was mitigated by the knowledge that Chinsoo and his sacrificed brethren were among the noble army of martyrs, victorious, resident in Light. I suspect he would have implied that the Communion of the Saints was richer because of Chinsoo's witness, although he probably would not have expressed it in those terms. He might have referred me to verses like these: "For as the sufferings of Christ abound in us, so our consolation also aboundeth by Christ" (2 Cor 1:5, KJV). "As ye are partakers of the sufferings of Christ, so shall ye be also of the consolation" (2 Cor 1:7, KJV).

His stand against idolatry never weakened, and he knew that the most dangerous idolatry was in everyday territories of the human heart, far removed from the question of Shinto shrines. Were he alive today, I am confident that once again he would challenge all Christians to identify with Chinsoo Kim and not bow down to a false god, no matter what form that false god might take, no matter what the seeming advantages, whether the worship be coerced from without or enticed from within.

But it's somewhat misleading for me to keep saying, "Were he alive today . . ."

The benefit I continue to draw from his ministry is not purely of remembrance. When in worship I am brought "to the souls of just men made perfect" ("With angels and archangels, and with all the company of heaven, we laud and magnify thy glorious Name, evermore praising thee and saying, Holy, Holy, Holy, Lord God of Hosts"), I sometimes call a silent roll of my strongest connections in that Church Triumphant. High on the list is Stanley Soltau.

His faith remains active in the lives of his offspring: Eleanor is a medical doctor serving the Lord in the Kingdom of Jordan; Mary recently retired from a ministry in food service in a center for the handicapped; George is involved in prison ministries on a full-time basis; Addison is Professor of Missions at Covenant Theological Seminary.

I rejoice with them in their heritage.

I still detect their father's voice in the reading of the Word. He sounds especially close in the doxologies of Saint Paul. I can hear him now:

"Now unto the king eternal, immortal, invisible, the only wise God, be honor and glory, for ever and ever. Amen."

Amen.

Alexander Solzhenitsyn

by Malcolm Muggeridge

I HAD THE GREAT PRIVILEGE of interviewing Alexander Solzhenitsyn in May 1983, when he was in London to receive the annual Templeton Award. The interview took place in a private house, not in a TV studio, which in my experience always gives a flavor of unreality to words uttered and thoughts expounded. Solzhenitsyn and I sat at ease in armchairs, and soon became unconscious of the cameras and other TV gear. Our interpreter, a Russian lady from Cambridge University, was wonderfully skillful, to the point that I soon had a sense of talking directly with Solzhenitsyn, without any intermediary. Of the interview itself I can only say that in a lifetime of journalism involving many interviews the one with Solzhenitsyn impressed me more than any of the others with the exception of Mother Teresa and General de Gaulle.

After Khrushchev took over in the Kremlin and abolished every

Note: Malcolm Muggeridge's interview with Alexander Solzhenitsyn was originally a BBC broadcast; an edited version of the interview was also published in the *Listener* in July 1983.

trace of Stalin, he amazed everyone by authorizing the publication of Solzhenitsyn's novel *One Day in the Life of Ivan Denisovich*, which gave a devastating account of life in the labor camps, or "Gulag Archipelago" as Solzhenitsyn called them. The book's enormous success opened the way for Solzhenitsyn, had he so wished, to follow the example of Maxim Gorky, and make his peace with the Soviet regime and enjoy its favors—in Gorky's case, among other things, it was a villa in Italy and the freedom to come and go. I have a vivid memory of Gorky in 1932, when I was the *Manchester Guardian* correspondent in Moscow, seeming to sleepwalk on and off platforms on public occasions, looking for all the world like a performing seal—which is precisely what he was.

In the circumstances Solzhenitsyn could scarcely be sent back to the labor camps, nor, after *One Day in the Life of Ivan Denisovich*, was he likely to produce books suitable for publication in the USSR. So the authorities, to his great distress, forcibly exiled him, and he settled in America, in Vermont, to undertake the task he had set himself—to stand by his fellow prisoners, the *zeks*, and to, as he puts it, restore Russia's history, which, ever since the revolution of 1917, has had a great hole in it.

Here too, had he so wished, he could have established himself as the leading anti-Soviet exile. Instead, he lambasted the USA almost as severely as the USSR; for instance in his much-abused Harvard speech, and, more loftily, in his warning of what may befall the Western World as a consequence of the feebleness and moral confusion of those who shape its policies and direct its purposes. In a BBC broadcast he says: "We have become hopelessly enmeshed in our slavish worship of all that is pleasant, all that is comfortable, all that is material—we worship things, we worship products." Our conversation likewise conveys his wisdom and his prescience. The script follows. . . .

MALCOLM MUGGERIDGE: *When your three books about the Gulag were published they had a terrific impact. But I have the impression that with the passage of time people think that the prison camps are a thing of the past. Whereas, in actual fact, they are still very much in operation.*

ALEXANDER SOLZHENITSYN: There was a moment in our history when it seemed as though the Gulag Archipelago was indeed becoming something of the past. But this was a very brief moment and a deceptive one. The Gulag is still alive. In terms of cruelty it has not changed. It simply employs other forms of cruelty, making use of certain technical innovations. But in terms of its actual dimension, the Gulag Archipelago is indeed now smaller. In the past, it encompassed fifteen or twenty million people at one time. Now, the US State Department conservatively estimates that it consists of over four million people. According to emigré organizations which actually count the number of camps in existence, the Gulag now encompasses about six to seven million people. What has reduced the population? Not the kindness of the Soviet leaders. The reduction is due to the fact that Stalin, in his day, made an enormous advance in terms of horror and cruelty. He annihilated people far beyond the numbers that he needed to annihilate. And that created an inertia of horror. Now, only very little pressure is required in order to produce the desired result.

Would it be true to say that the free labor which the Gulag provides is an essential element in the Soviet economy?

This free labor has always been and still is essential. It is particularly used to accomplish jobs that no one else is willing to do, such as working with radioactive material where no protection is provided. Gulag labor is used to obtain radioactive material and to clean radioactive parts on submarines. These people, of course, die within a few months.

Do you think it possible that the Gulag apparatus could be removed from the Soviet regime without some violent upheaval in the USSR?

Violence is inherent in the communist system. The Gulag is an extreme manifestation of this violence. But there is a whole gradation of violence; so really your question should be turned round in this way: is communist totalitarianism possible without violence? The answer is no, not for one single day.

That makes it absolutely clear. In the US and the USSR there have been vast build-ups of nuclear weapons. Is it possible to imagine, given this situation, that we shall avoid nuclear war?

For some reason, I am convinced that there will be no nuclear war. There can be various explanations of why this conflict will not take place. If only, after 1945, the West had not disarmed itself, had not let all its armed forces disband but had retained conventional forces, then today there would be no danger of a nuclear confrontation. I won't go through all the possibilities, but I will consider one, and it is a very, very pessimistic variant. It is a possibility that arises as a result of ten years of concessions and capitulation. One of the reasons why there will not be a nuclear conflict is that the West has given in on the nuclear balance and has lost any kind of initiative in a balance of conventional forces. It is, therefore, very unprepared for subversion from within. Even without recourse to nuclear confrontation, there are all sorts of possibilities for the communist leaders.

I am a very old journalist, and people often ask me what I consider to be the most interesting or significant thing that has happened in the last fifty years. I tell them that the most important event is the revival of the Christian faith in the one place in the world where I would have expected it to have no chance of reviving. Would it be true to say that the efforts of the Soviet authorities to prevent any faith in Christianity or practice of the Christian religion has been a failure?

What you have said has a profound significance. For the last five or six decades all we have seen in many places in the world is the victory of communism. True, these are victories which don't really bring much good to people. They are not economic victories; they are not good, positive victories. They are really victories of power. In our country, the communist powers took military steps against the Christian faith. The signal for an attack against Christianity was given right at the very beginning by Lenin and Trotsky. The secret political police were mobilized against the faith. Millions of peasants were slaughtered in order to eradicate faith from the very roots of the people. Millions of hours of propaganda time were used in order to burn out faith from the hearts of the children. Yet, despite all that, we can say that after all these years communism has not destroyed the Christian faith. Christianity went through a period of decline, but now it is growing and reviving. That is the most hopeful sign that one can see anywhere, not only in my country, but anywhere in the world.

For the moment I see no end to the military victories of communism. It looks as though the shadow of communism is covering the earth more and more deeply. It is like an eclipse of the sun. But in an eclipse only a small portion of the earth is darkened, whereas with communism, it is half the earth which is in darkness, maybe even three-quarters. But because communism has already shown its weakness, its inability to destroy Christianity, we may hope that its shadow will gradually pass across and clear the earth. It will perhaps clear precisely those countries which have been in the deepest shadow until now.

It is amazing that Dostoevsky saw all this at least 100 years ago. Not only that, but he saw in The Devils *that the demon that would bring it all about was the demon of liberalism. I always think that you are rather like Dostoevsky.*

I never stop wondering, never stop marveling at the prophetic power, the prophetic vision of Dostoevsky. We already see happening what he foresaw in many parts of the world. But it is amazing that he saw the very first beginnings and sometimes even perceived things that had not yet begun in his time. When we think about our own times, it is amazing how often we return to Dostoevsky and can only marvel at how accurately he foresaw everything.

Dostoevsky wasn't supposed to be read in the Soviet Union. But now they've revived him. The fascinating thing to me, the most amazing ideological acrobatics that I've ever seen, is that they're trying to persuade us that Dostoevsky was a hangover from Karl Marx and that even Lenin, though he spoke severely about him, admired him.

There is no end to Marxist acrobatics. It's not only Dostoevsky who communists have, so to speak, colonized as an ally, but while attacking Christianity, they are ready to colonize our Lord Jesus Christ as well. The political atheist literature, in fact, maintains that Marxism continues what Christianity began, that it makes possible what Christianity failed to achieve. If this were only limited to the communist countries.... But this trick, this sleight of hand, we find throughout the world, because socialists everywhere constantly ascribe Christian virtues to themselves. Socialism is, in fact, absolutely opposed to Christianity. Christianity is founded on good will; whereas socialism is founded on violence or, if you like, on pressure. Nonetheless, socialism constantly tries to appear in a Christian guise, attempting to exploit what is, in fact, Christian.

Do you ever expect to go back to Russia?

In a strange way, I am inwardly absolutely convinced that I shall go back. I live with this simple conviction: I shall go back. I mean my own personal physical return, not just a return through my books. Now that contradicts any rational assumption. I am not so young and I can't point to any actual facts which make me say this. History is so full of unexpected things that some of the simplest facts in our lives we cannot foretell in advance.

You have lived in the West for several years. Do you think that we are fated to be swallowed up in this thing—that there will be a complete disintegration of our Christian civilization?

The threat is very much alive, very much present. If one were to speak merely of the simple advance, the push of communism, yes, it is very possible that communism may come to obscure the West. But, by the same law of the eclipse of the sun, the shadow shall pass. The West may escape this destiny, this fate. Maybe the West still has several decades of development before it. But if the West does not find in itself the spiritual forces, the spiritual strength to rise again, to find itself again, then, yes, Christian civilization will disintegrate. We use the same words to describe the same phenomenon: democracy. Democracy was originally developed before the face of God. And the foundation of its concept of equality was equality before God. But then the image of God receded, was pushed away by man. And this same democracy changed and acquired a very strange character. What is now demanded is an equality that favors mediocrity. The responsibility that each person had before God, this concept of responsibility has been lost. Whereas the so-called democratic institutions cannot exercise any force, any pressure. And so, having lost any concept of true responsibility, we are, so to speak, free to destroy our institutions and ourselves.

Do you think that the situation, then, is hopeless?

Thank God, and I mean thank God, the situation is never hopeless. In the USSR, you might say that we have lost everything and yet our position is not hopeless. I do not consider that human history has reached its ultimate point. The measures that we use are far too small, too short to really measure. The history of the decline of Christian civilization, the history of communism which has come into the world—all this will be measured in sections, but history will continue. The lesson that we—mankind, humanity—have to learn takes many centuries to learn.

I've thought about it a lot, and I've thought this: when we say Western civilization, we mean Christendom. And therefore we could say that Christendom is finished, but not Christ.

No, I would not like to take it upon myself to say that the social form of Christian life has gone forever. It may be that there are possibilities of change or development which we simply don't know about. And indeed, if it were not still present, then Christianity would be something that would be removed from us. It would, so to speak, ascend to the heavens. I think we shall see many forms of Christianity on earth.

I have heard that you feel it a duty to give Russia back its history.

As a writer it is my duty to speak in the name, not only of those who are in the Gulag and who died in the Gulag, but also in the name of those who died in the revolution. Yes, it is my aim to return to Russia the memory of its past. I have been working on this for forty-seven years. And in my work I have discovered that the year 1917 offers an extraordinarily compressed summary of the whole history of the twentieth century. The eight months from February to October 1917 in Russia are like an accelerated film. Now the film is being replayed in slow-motion throughout the whole world. I did not set out with the intention of explaining that to the world. My original aim was simply to return to Russia its own memory. But in the last few years, now that I have completed a number of volumes, I see that I have been writing something of the history of the whole twentieth century.

I was first in Russia as a young journalist in 1932-33. At that time everybody adulated Stalin in an utterly extravagant way, including many distinguished western authors. Then came Khrushchev's speech at the Twentieth Party Congress. Suddenly all the busts of Stalin were removed, the statues were taken away. It was time to abolish Stalin. Do you think that they'll ever put him back?

There isn't really a need for this any more. It's enough simply to have the two models, Lenin and Marx. If there are too many in between, then the significance, the importance of the originals is diminished.

What about the ordinary Russian people? They are given this extraordinary idea of Stalin, this great man. Then they wake up one morning and hear he is not a great man after all. Do they start to think that perhaps his successor is not a great man either? Does it destroy their confidence?

Here, I think, for the Western mind, history has been written inaccurately. Even in the thirties, I knew scores of people who had absolutely no respect for Stalin. In the villages, it was the most uneducated, the simplest people. So really, the sort of dethronement of Stalin was no event and no surprise to them. It was a shock at the highest levels of the Soviet intelligentsia, for the communist elite, and for the so-called progressive western circles who actually believed in Stalin. Khrushchev's speech at the Twentieth Party Congress only opened the eyes of those who had willfully deceived themselves. In the camps we all shouted hooray when we heard that Stalin had died. Those who wept were the young fourteen- and fifteen-year-old girls in the communist youth movement.

I've always been very interested in underground publishing in the USSR, what is called the samizdat. *Are your books coming out through the* samizdat?

In the Soviet Union, *samizdat* is the dissemination of texts by the person, or by the people who have actually written them. To this day various sort of declarations and statements are made through *samizdat* and distributed through *samizdat*. Serious works of research in religion and in philosophy, for example, are also distributed through *samizdat*. When I was still living in the Soviet Union, there was quite a lively distribution of literary work through *samizdat*. Two of my novels, *The First Circle* and *Cancer*

Ward, were very widely distributed and read precisely through *samizdat.* But when I began being widely published in the West, people preferred to try and get one of those editions. Yes, my books do penetrate into the Soviet Union, though not in enormous numbers, but they certainly do penetrate. Every book is read by perhaps fifty to sixty people. For example, whenever someone's flat is searched, among the objects found will be a book of mine. It means an enormous amount to me to know that my books do get to Russian readers and that they are available there.

You've been living in America. Have you been dreaming the American dream?

In America I was able to realize that which I had always dreamed about—that all my life should be a life of work. In the Soviet Union I could never devote myself entirely to literature. I had to earn my livelihood by some other means. Also, I could never keep all my books or all that I had written in my own flat, in my own house. At any moment, whether day or night, I had to expect a search by the KGB. So every evening I had to think, now where shall I hide this? I kept so few manuscripts within reach that sometimes when I had to compare two sections, say two texts of the *Gulag Archipelago,* I couldn't do so, because one or the other of them wasn't there. And I had hardly any access to a library. And, of course, emigré editions were totally inaccessible. Whereas now, I have five or six tables full of manuscripts and books. My life from early morning till late at night consists of working on my writing. No exception is made for any holidays or journeys anywhere. And I really do feel that at last I am doing that for which I was born, But all this is, so to speak, illumined by the sun, the light that is my hope of returning to my country.

Solzhenitsyn and the Consensus

It has fascinated me to see how the media have decided to go after Solzhenitsyn because he has not played the Emigre Game as they consider it should be played. Instead of gratefully finding himself in what we still call the Free World and being duly thankful, he has ventured to point out that the Free World is not really a Free World at all, and that freedom is not what it purports to be in our so-called Free World.

What has given the consensus people the feeling that Solzhenitsyn was not after all their particular hero has been his insistence that what he is concerned about much more than ideologies is Christianity. Furthermore, he has stated that the only way in which Russia can find its way back to a real existence is through Christ, and that his answer to the Gulag Archipelago is Christianity, not liberalism. This goes dead against consensus considerations—a man brought up in the USSR, and coming from a labor camp, stands up and says that the answer to it all has nothing to do with "One Man, One Vote!"; it has everything to do with Christ.

All kinds of criticisms have been developed. For instance, articles are written suggesting that Solzhenitsyn wants to re-establish Tsarism, which is nonsensical. What he does say is that men are not made free by being allowed, and having the means, to do what they like. In the second Gulag book, in a chapter called "The Ascent," he says that it was in the prison camp that he learnt what freedom is, and that the line between Good and Evil runs, not between countries, not between classes, not between political parties, but down each separate individual heart. And he adds: "Thank you, camps, for teaching me this truth." Then there are the subversives who want to believe that there is a possible compromise between the so-called Free World and the communist world—as it might be vegetarians and the Worshipful Company of Butchers seated together on the same platform.

To me Solzenitsyn is like a projection of Dostoevsky, whom he even somewhat resembles. Some years ago, on the occasion of the centenary of Dostoevsky's death, I went to the USSR to do the commentary for a TV program on him. It came as a surprise that anything of the kind should be permitted; ever since the Revolution he had been anathema and his works suppressed, but now the ban has been lifted, and he is once again a popular and greatly admired author, despite his anti-Marxist and anti-revolutionary attitudes. To bring about this change, the most amazing dialectical acrobatics were required. Almost the last thing Dostoevsky did was to deliver an extraordinary address at the unveiling of a Pushkin Memorial in 1880, which delighted all the so-called reactionary elements in Tsarist Russia. When we were recording our program and came to Dostoevsky's great oration, I found myself walking about the streets where the Pushkin Memorial stood, and echoing the English translation of Dostoevsky's speech. Somehow, although no one could understand them, they boded good.

More clearly than any other commentator in the world today Solzhenitsyn sees the dangers that encompass us all. In a murky time he represents what is noble and wonderful in human life. A very great man.

Other Books of Interest from Servant Publications

Bright Legacy
Portraits of Ten Outstanding Christian Women
Edited by Ann Spangler

In one volume, ten of today's most prominent Christian women write affectionately about their heroes. Contributors include Elisabeth Elliot, Kitty Muggeridge, Karen Burton Mains, Rebecca Pippert, Ingrid Trobisch, and Madeleine L'Engle. (paperback) *$6.95*

Learning to Walk Alone
Personal Reflections on a Time of Grief
By Ingrid Trobisch

In this touching memoir, Ingrid Trobisch shares about how she dealt with the sudden death of her beloved husband Walter. She provides counsel, encouragement, and hope for anyone who knows what it means to lose a loved one. (hardcover) *$8.95*

A Lamp for My Feet
Reflections on Life with God
By Elisabeth Elliot

Insightful reflections on scripture from one of today's most respected Christian authors. (hardcover) *$9.95*

Available at your Christian bookstore or from
**Servant Publications • Dept. 209 • P.O. Box 7455
Ann Arbor, Michigan 48107**
Please include payment plus $1.00 for postage
when ordering by mail.
Send for your FREE catalog of books, music, cassettes.

ϒ